JAMES HOGG

Selected Poems

JAMES HOGG, AGED 60
From the portrait in *Altrive Tales*, 1832

JAMES HOGG

Selected Poems

EDITED BY

DOUGLAS S. MACK

OXFORD
AT THE CLARENDON PRESS
1970

Oxford University Press, Ely House, London W. 1

GLASGOW NEW YORK TORONTO MELBOURNE WELLINGTON
CAPE TOWN SALISBURY IBADAN NAIROBI DAR ES SALAAM LUSAKA ADDIS ABABA
BOMBAY CALCUTTA MADRAS KARACHI LAHORE DACCA
KUALA LUMPUR SINGAPORE HONG KONG TOKYO

PRINTED IN GREAT BRITAIN

FOR WILMA

PREFACE

HOGG wrote a large quantity of verse, but a substantial proportion of his poems are undistinguished. As a result, the sheer volume of his unsuccessful verse has tended to submerge his important work, and the significance of his poetry has not been widely recognized. It is hoped that the publication of this selection of Hogg's best poems will make possible a revaluation of his stature as a poet.

Something should perhaps be said about the selection which has been made from *The Queen's Wake*, Hogg's best-known book of verse. This work is in fact a collection of poems linked together by a narrative framework concerning a festival of poetry held in honour of Mary Queen of Scots. The pieces included in the collection are of a very uneven quality, but two of them—'Kilmeny' and 'The Witch of Fife'—are without doubt Hogg's most important poems. These two poems have been included in this selection, together with the 'Introduction' to *The Queen's Wake* and other appropriate parts of the linking narrative. This method of selection allows 'Kilmeny' and 'The Witch of Fife' to be read in the context which Hogg intended for them.

The Introduction to the present volume consists mainly of a critical evaluation of Hogg's achievement as a poet. If an editor is introducing a collection of largely unknown and unread poems to the public, it seems clear that his first duty is to explain why he believes that these poems are worthy of attention. Hogg's quite remarkable life is of particular interest to students of his poetry, and a concise statement of the main biographical facts has been given in the Chronology.

A number of Hogg's poems were extensively revised by the author. These revisions are discussed in the Commentary, where an outline of the history of the text of each poem is also given. Many of the early editions contain notes by Hogg, and these are reprinted with the texts of the poems. Where necessary, further annotation has been provided in the Commentary.

As I am myself a librarian, it gives me particular pleasure to acknowledge the debt which all editors owe to members of my profession. I am especially grateful to my colleagues in St. Andrews University Library, and to my former colleagues in the National Library of Scotland, for the efficiency with which they have dealt with my many requests. My thanks are also due to Professor G. Ross Roy, editor of *Studies in Scottish Literature*, for permission to reprint in the Introduction material on 'Kilmeny' which first appeared in that journal; and to the Trustees of the National Library of Scotland for permission to quote in the Commentary from the Hogg manuscripts in that library.

This volume owes a great deal to the advice and encouragement of Dr. W. R. Aitken, of the University of Strathclyde's Department of Librarianship, and I would like to record my especial gratitude to him. My thanks are also due to many other people for advice, information, and help of various kinds. I would like to mention particularly A. Bell, Miss H. Buchan, I. M. Campbell, R. G. Ferguson, K. C. Fraser, the Revd. D. Guthrie, R. D. S. Jack, J. Kidd, Miss M. Lochhead, D. Low, S. McMinn, K. McG. Mack, R. V. Pringle, and R. N. Smart. Errors and faulty judgements in the book are of course entirely my own.

Finally, I would like to thank my wife for all the help and advice she has given me in the preparation of this volume.

CONTENTS

—————

INTRODUCTION

———

For a period of almost a century it was customary for critics writing on James Hogg to dismiss him, either with faint praise or with no praise at all. Nevertheless, he has now come to be regarded as a writer of major importance. The renewal of interest in Hogg began in 1947 when his novel, *The Private Memoirs and Confessions of a Justified Sinner*, was republished with an enthusiastic introduction by André Gide. Gide tells us that he first read the novel 'with a stupefaction and admiration that increased at every page', and other critics, including David Daiches, Kurt Wittig, Edwin Eigner, and Walter Allen,[1] have followed him in giving the *Private Memoirs* high praise.

It would be fair to say, however, that it is only Hogg the novelist who has been re-established as a major figure. Hogg the poet remains neglected, in spite of the high reputation he achieved in his own lifetime, and in spite of the fact that his poetry earned him the friendship and respect of men of the stature of Scott, Wordsworth, and Byron. In view of all this, a re-examination of Hogg's achievement as a poet seems to be overdue.[2]

---

[1] David Daiches, 'The Writing of Scottish Literary History', *Literary Essays* (Edinburgh and London, 1956), p. 150; Kurt Wittig, *The Scottish Tradition in Literature* (Edinburgh and London, 1958), pp. 247–9; Edwin M. Eigner, *Robert Louis Stevenson and Romantic Tradition* (Princeton, 1966), pp. 24–6. Walter E. Allen, *The English Novel* (London, 1954), pp. 124–5.

[2] There are interesting but brief discussions of Hogg's poetry in Wittig's *Scottish Tradition in Literature* and in John W. Oliver's essay on the earlier nineteenth century in *Scottish Poetry: a Critical Survey*, edited by James Kinsley (London, 1955). Louis Simpson's *James Hogg: a Critical Study* (Edinburgh and London, 1962) concentrates mainly on the prose,

The main reason for the present neglect of Hogg's poetry is clear: he wrote far too much verse, and his best poems have long been submerged among his failures. The present edition attempts to remove this barrier between the reader and Hogg's best work by collecting as many as possible of his successful poems into a single manageable volume.

Hogg's prolixity was not of course the only reason for his long period of neglect. Another factor was undoubtedly the reputation he acquired as a boor and a buffoon, a mere rustic clown who could not possibly be taken seriously as a writer. There is evidence that Hogg's public behaviour was sometimes eccentric and extravagant, but equally there is no doubt that his trait was exaggerated and caricatured by some of his contemporaries. Hogg's reputation as 'the boar of the forest' was based to a considerable extent on the very much larger-than-life portrait of him in John Wilson's 'Noctes Ambrosianae'. The 'Noctes', which appeared regularly in *Blackwood's Magazine* from 1822 till 1835, purported to be reproductions of the table-talk of the Blackwood group of writers, including Hogg in the character of the 'Ettrick Shepherd'.[1] Hogg soon became identified in the public mind with Wilson's conceited, hard-drinking, quaint rustic, even although Lockhart in 1831 vigorously denied in the *Quarterly Review* that he was the 'boozing buffoon' portrayed in the 'Noctes'.[2]

and the discussion of the poetry is to a large extent descriptive rather than critical. A detailed critical re-examination of Hogg's poetry has not yet been published.

[1] The 'Noctes' were probably sometimes based on actual conversations, but there is no doubt that they were to a large extent the product of Wilson's imagination. Some numbers were by writers other than Wilson, and Hogg himself contributed; nevertheless, Wilson was responsible for the bulk of the 'Noctes'.

[2] *Quarterly Review*, vol. 44 (1831), p. 82. Lockhart's view is supported by Hogg's daughter, Mrs. Garden, in her *Memorials of James Hogg* (Paisley, 1903), pp. 139–40. Mrs. Garden writes that her mother was so moved by some passages in the 'Noctes' that they made 'her pulse beat faster and her eye sparkle with a wife's indignation'. Mrs. Garden herself adds that the Shepherd of the 'Noctes' was not 'the Shepherd his own home knew'.

Wilson did not create the figure of the Shepherd unaided,
however. Hogg himself played his part, by adopting the
Shepherd as a kind of public pose, comparable to Burns's
impersonation of the 'Heaven-taught Ploughman'. Both
men, being peasants, found it necessary to adopt a defen-
sive mask when they came in contact with the sophisticated
society of Edinburgh.[1]

Hogg's background was a remarkable one for an eminent
man of letters, and an understanding of it will explain why
Wilson's picture of him gained its currency. Hogg was
born in 1770 in a remote part of Ettrick Forest in the
Borders. He had only a few months' schooling, family
circumstances making it necessary for most of his childhood
to be spent in farm service, and, as a result, when he
reached the age of eighteen he was only semi-literate. He
then began the formidable task of self-education, and it is
clear from his own works that he became familiar with
many of the older masterpieces of both Scottish and
English literature, as well as with the works of his con-
temporaries. Imitations of the style of Pope and Milton
appear in his longer poems, for example, and his *Poetic
Mirror* contains brilliant parodies of Wordsworth, Scott,
and Byron, among others. All in all, we need not be sur-
prised that Lockhart could call Hogg 'a laborious and
successful student'.[2]

Even though Hogg came to his book-learning late, his
childhood had great compensations. His mother had an
exceptional knowledge of the old ballads and of Border
folklore and superstitions. Hogg was steeped in these things
from his earliest days, and in addition he acquired from his
pious father a wide knowledge of the Bible and an intimate

---

[1] The 'polite' culture of Edinburgh in Hogg's period and before is dis-
cussed in David Craig's *Scottish Literature and the Scottish People, 1680–
1830* (London, 1961). In this important book Dr. Craig sets out to examine
'the essentials of Scottish culture during the period, in relation to the
literature and its public'.   [2] *Quarterly Review*, vol. 44 (1831), p. 82.

understanding of the religious life of Scotland. These child-
hood influences show themselves again and again in his
best work.

Much of what is worst in his writing can also be traced,
although indirectly, to the influence of his background. When
Hogg, the self-educated shepherd, established his reputation
as a writer and came into contact with the sophisticated
literary world of Edinburgh, the predictable consequence
was that he accepted too uncritically the validity of Edin-
burgh's opinions and fashions. As a result, many of his works
are simply attempts to produce the kind of writing that he
thought Edinburgh would admire—and this is one of the main
reasons for the existence of the large body of unsuccessful
verse which has done so much harm to his reputation.

A particularly clear example of this tendency is provided
by the many poems which Hogg wrote in imitation of the
style of M. G. Lewis, who is now best remembered as the
author of 'The Monk'. Lewis's verse, which was one of
the more eccentric by-products of the Romantic movement,
was admired by Byron, Scott, and other important figures.
In spite of this his poems are little more than sensational
horror stories, and their reputation did not survive for long.
For instance, Lewis's most famous poem, 'Alonzo the Brave
and the Fair Imogene', is simply an attempt to generate
terror by describing the sudden appearance of the rotting
corpse of a knight, who has returned from the dead to
accuse his faithless lover at her bridal feast.

'Young Kennedy', one of the poems from Hogg's *Queen's
Wake*, also depends for its effect on the horrific appearance
of a wronged ghost on the occasion of a marriage, and
there are many other examples in Hogg's work of the kind
of Gothic terror purveyed by Lewis.[1] As we shall see, Hogg

[1] Gothic poems by Hogg include 'Glen-Avin', 'MacGregor', 'King
Edward's Dream', and 'The Lord of Balloch'. Gothic passages also occur
in his long narrative poems, notably in 'Mador of the Moor' and 'Queen
Hynde'.

was interested in the supernatural, but it is unfortunate that this interest, together with a desire to please Edinburgh, caused him to devote so much of his energy to the production of poems of this kind.

Apart from his determination to follow literary fashions the chief reason for Hogg's large output of bad verse was his diffuseness, of which 'Mary Scott', another of the songs from *The Queen's Wake*, is an example. Hogg tells us in a note that his poem is founded on the old ballad 'The Gay Goss-Hawk', but while the ballad is only 156 lines long,[1] Hogg's poem takes 732 lines to tell substantially the same story. What is worse, 'Mary Scott' loses in the process all of the ballad's drama and emotional power.

Most of Hogg's best poetry was written when his object was to please himself rather than Edinburgh. Thus his many excellent songs make no concessions to the taste of genteel society, but are rather written in the spirit of the traditional folk-songs he knew as a child in Ettrick Forest.

Hogg's work as a song-writer has been overshadowed by the pre-eminence of Burns in the same field, but his achievement is nevertheless considerable. In particular, his pastoral songs and many of his love songs are remarkable for the mood of calm and tranquil twilight beauty which they evoke. Outstanding among these are 'When the Kye Comes Hame', and 'O Jeannie there's Naethin tae Fear Ye'.

Hogg also wrote many comic songs. One of the best of these is about 'The Village of Balmaquhapple', which is 'steeped in iniquity up to the thrapple', and whose inhabitants include

> Geordie our deacon, for want of a better,
> An, Bess, wha delights in the sins that beset her.

The whole song is written with great exuberance, and is an outstanding piece of extravagant and grotesque satire.

---

[1] In the version in Scott's *Minstrelsy of the Scottish Border.*

'The Lass of Carlisle' provides comedy of a quieter kind. The heroine of this song is beautiful and wealthy, fortune's favourite in every way. In time she marries, and has

> plenty o' weans,
> That keepit her hands astir;
> And then she dee'd and was buried,
> An' there was an end of her.

Hogg's war-songs, however, were his outstanding contribution to the tradition of Scottish song. Poems like 'Donald MacDonald', 'Bonnie Prince Charlie', and especially 'Lock the Door, Lariston' are remarkable for their vigorous and intricate rhythmical and alliterative patterns. These songs must be read aloud if Hogg's mastery of this kind of effect is to be appreciated.

Most of Hogg's songs are written in Scots, a fact which influences their character greatly. Even apart from the many differences in vocabulary, the distinctive rhythms, idioms, and connotations of Scots give that language a quite different texture from English. Scots was of course the language of Hogg's childhood, and the colloquial freshness and vigour of many of his songs can be attributed to his thorough familiarity with the rich spoken Scots of Ettrick Forest. Hogg habitually spoke Scots throughout his life, and as a result he was able to write in Scots instinctively and unselfconsciously—an advantage which his successors have not always shared.

In addition to his original songs, Hogg, like Ramsay and Burns before him, did valuable work as a collector and reviser of traditional material. For instance, he wrote a lively new version of 'Charlie is my Darling', and in such songs as 'McLean's Welcome' and 'O Jeannie there's Naething tae Fear Ye' he provided new words for old tunes. As a song collector, Hogg made a significant contribution to Scott's *Minstrelsy of the Scottish Border*, and his own two volumes of *Jacobite Relics* are a valuable source of traditional song material.

The old ballads were an important part of the folk-poetry which Hogg knew as a child, and they influenced his own poetry deeply. Unfortunately, however, most of his attempts to copy the ballad style were less successful than his work in the folk-song tradition. Many of his ballads fail because, like 'Mary Scott', they are too long and diffuse, but nevertheless in some poems, and in particular 'The Mermaid', he does achieve the economy of expression and the tragic understatement of the ballads.

It would be wrong, however, to imagine that Hogg wrote successful verse only when he worked within the limits of the folk-poetry of Ettrick Forest. On the contrary, we find him in his Edinburgh years excelling in the highly sophisticated art of poetic parody. Indeed, his *Poetic Mirror* has been called by George Kitchin 'one of the more considerable books of parodies in our language'.[1] Many of Hogg's contemporaries figure in *The Poetic Mirror*, but the most successful pieces are 'James Rigg' and 'The Flying Tailor', both parodies of Wordsworth. In 'James Rigg' the brilliance of the opening is not maintained, but both works present, with slight but pointed exaggerations, every quirk and mannerism of Wordsworth's less inspired moments:

> underneath a stunted yew,
> Some three yards distant from the gravel-walk,
> On the left-hand side, thou wilt espy a grave,
> With unelaborate headstone beautified,

We also find Hogg going beyond the tradition of folk-poetry in several works which show the influence of the old Makars. A reasonably wide selection of the masterpieces of

---

[1] George Kitchin, *A Survey of Burlesque and Parody in English* (Edinburgh and London, 1931), p. 214. *The Poetic Mirror*, of course, took its place in a flourishing tradition of poetic parody, a tradition which also produced *Rejected Addresses*, by James and Horatio Smith (1812).

medieval Scottish poetry was available to him in antholo-
gies like Pinkerton's *Ancient Scotish Poems*, Ramsay's
Evergreen, and Sibbald's *Chronicle of Ancient Scottish
Poetry*,[1] and Hogg frequently follows an ancient Scottish
tradition by adopting the *a b a b: b c b c* stanza for poems of
grave reflection.[2] He achieves a level of deep seriousness
in some of these poems, and especially in 'Superstition',
'St Mary of the Lows', and 'The Monitors'. 'Superstition'
is of particular interest as it is a meditation on a recurring
theme of Hogg's work both in poetry and prose—his
complex and ambiguous attitude towards the supernatural
and the cult of witchcraft.

Some of Hogg's reflective poems are written in English,
while others contain comparatively few Scots usages. This
is not surprising, as a form of standard English derived
largely from the Authorized Version of the Bible has been
used since the Reformation in Scots-speaking communities
for the discussion of religious matters. As a result, speakers
of Scots in Hogg's period tended to turn instinctively to
English when they wished to achieve a serious, lofty, or
religious tone. Thus in 'Kilmeny' Hogg's language is much
closer to standard English in the scenes in heaven than in
the scenes on earth—a variation that can be seen even in the
first version of the poem, although here it is concealed behind
mock-antique spellings. Many of the movements between
Scots and English in Hogg's poetry mirror in a similar way
the fluctuations of post-Reformation Scottish speech.

Hogg was familiar from his infancy with standard
English as well as with Scots. His father—a devout Kirk
elder—frequently read passages of the Bible to the family,

---

[1] In this context, it is perhaps worth remarking that, in a note on one
of his own poems, Hogg discusses Dunbar's 'Lament for the Makaris'.
See *The Works of The Ettrick Shepherd*, edited by T. Thompson (London,
1865), vol. 2, p. 57.

[2] See Wittig, p. 246. This stanza form is used in such poems as 'The
Thre Deid Pollis' by Henryson and 'The Tabill of Confession' by Dunbar.

and from his mother's recitation he learned by heart the entire Scottish Metrical Psalter, of which he later wrote— 'my veneration of our ancient psalmody is such, that to see an innovation in it would almost break my heart'.[1] Hogg's outstanding poems are written in Scots, but he could write successful English verse, as in 'Superstition', 'St Mary of the Lows', and the 'Introduction' of *The Queen's Wake*. His English tends to become unconvincing and stiff, however, when he attempts to emulate (rather than parody) the English style of other poets. For example 'Mador of the Moor', 'Pilgrims of the Sun', and 'Queen Hynde' contain long pedestrian passages in which he adopts in turn the manner of the Augustans, of Milton, and of Scott.

As we have already seen, Hogg's poetry shows traces of contact with the work of the medieval Scottish Makars. Henryson's 'Robin and Makene' is one of the poems included in the collections of Ramsay and Sibbald, and it seems probable that this work influenced Hogg's 'Ringan and May', another pastoral dialogue between two lovers. At any rate Hogg's work, in its quiet, humorous, and perceptive observation of human nature, has at least some of the qualities of Henryson's poem.

Of course, Hogg's interest in traditional Scottish folk-poetry and in the medieval Makars was shared by Ramsay, Fergusson, and Burns, his three great predecessors in the eighteenth century. Indeed, the poems we have considered so far can be regarded as a successful continuation of the traditions of the eighteenth-century revival of Scottish poetry, and this achievement alone would entitle Hogg to an important place in Scottish literary history. In addition, we still have to consider 'Kilmeny' and 'The Witch of Fife', the poems on which Hogg's claim to our consideration chiefly rests. In view of their importance, it is necessary to examine these works in some detail.

[1] *Edinburgh Literary Journal* (1830), vol. 3, p. 163.

Both are included in *The Queen's Wake*, a collection of poems within a narrative framework concerning a festival of poetry held in honour of Mary Queen of Scots. *The Queen's Wake* includes 'Young Kennedy', 'Mary Scott', and several other undistinguished poems, and taken as a whole it is a failure. However, this does not detract from the importance of the best poems in the collection.

'The Witch of Fife' begins with an account of the nocturnal exploits of a group of witches, and Hogg draws on his deep knowledge and understanding of the peasant superstitions he knew as a child in Ettrick to give to their adventures an air of awesome majesty:

> Quhite, quhite was ouir rode, that was never trode,
> Owr the snawis of eternity!

The poem continues with an account of how the husband of one of the witches contrives to join them in one of their revels in the Bishop of Carlisle's wine-cellars. Once there, he drinks himself to a standstill with an exuberant delight. The old man is a superb creation, as inexorably this-worldly as Sancho Panza himself, and the incongruity of the contrast between him and the awesome world of the witches produces a grotesque comedy of the highest order.

Hogg shows considerable skill in maintaining a balance between the two sides of his wild contrast. The magnificently unheroic old man is kept very much in the background until the grandeur of the witches has been firmly established; if this had not been the case, the reader would have found it impossible to take the witches very seriously. Equally, Hogg takes care to prepare the reader for the mood of the second section of the poem by allowing the old man to make one or two characteristic comments on the opening account of the witches' journeyings. Thus when his wife tells him that 'our beauty blumit like the Lapland rose', her gallant husband replies:

Ye lee, ye lee, ye ill womyne,
Se loud as I heir ye lee!
For the warst-faurd wyfe on the shoris of Fyfe
Is cumlye comparet wi' thee.

'The Witch of Fife' is written in a kind of pseudo-antique Scots used by Hogg more than once. This language is clearly an imitation of the Middle Scots of the old Makars, and indeed Hogg's first poem of this kind—published in 1811 in *The Spy*, no. 48—is entitled 'Antient Fragment, Copied from an Old Ms'. Hogg gives his language an air of antiquity mainly by means of spelling—*quh-* for *wh-*, *-it* for *-ed*, and so on—and poems like 'The Witch of Fife' do not reproduce Middle Scots accurately. Nevertheless they emphasize Hogg's interest in the medieval Makars, and his readiness to enrich his Scots from literary sources. 'Kilmeny' and 'Ringan and May' were first published in Hogg's archaic language, but he later 'translated' these poems into a more modern Scots. Although it provides an appropriate vehicle for the outlandish absurdities of 'The Witch of Fife', Hogg's archaic language added nothing to his other poems except unnecessary obscurity.

The 'Witch of Fife' is rooted in the distinctive feeling of the old Scottish peasantry for the supernatural, a feeling which Lord David Cecil has described as being 'at once homely and Gothic, earthy and fantastic, at times grotesquely comic but shot through with an authentic thrill of super-natural terror'.[1] These words refer specifically to Scott's 'Wandering Willie's Tale', but there could be no more accurate description of the contrasting moods of Hogg's poem.

Needless to say, the tradition of Scottish popular diablerie which produced 'Wandering Willie's Tale' and 'The Witch of Fife' also lies behind Burns's 'Tam o' Shanter', a poem which Hogg admired greatly, and which clearly

[1] Sir Walter Scott, *Short Stories*, with an Introduction by Lord David Cecil (London, 1934), p. xvi.

influenced 'The Witch of Fife'. In particular, Hogg's old man is highly reminiscent of Burns's hero. 'The Witch of Fife' also owes a great deal to the ballad tradition, from which Hogg took his stanza form and various mannerisms of phraseology:

> Away, away, ye ill womyne,
> An ill deide met ye dee!

Nevertheless, it is very much an original and personal poem. Hogg inherited from his childhood a genuine feeling for the terror of the supernatural, yet in his writings he frequently shows a desire to poke fun at peasant superstitions. In 'The Witch of Fife' he combined these two impulses successfully, and thus produced a magnificent piece of high comedy.

In 'Kilmeny' Hogg's achievement is even more remarkable. This poem has been praised by many critics for its calm and tranquil beauty, but none of them has justly interpreted its full significance. A majority of the critics have based their readings on an assumption of questionable validity—the assumption that 'Kilmeny' is one of Hogg's many poems about fairies.[1] In fact, an examination of the text suggests that the poem's heroine, Kilmeny, is not taken to fairyland as the critics assume, but to heaven. In the words of the poem she is taken to

> That land to human spirits given,
> The lowermost vales of the storied heaven;
> From thence they can view the world below,
> And heaven's blue gates with sapphires glow,
> More glory yet unmeet to know.

---

[1] W. L. Renwick, in *English Literature 1789–1815* (vol. 9 of the *Oxford History of English Literature*, Oxford, 1963), p. 220, calls the poem 'a fairy-tale that is neither a museum-piece nor a Shakespearian prettiness'. Other typical opinions are: 'The Land of Fairy was, as I have said, Hogg's peculiar domain; and "Kilmeny" is his finest picture of it' (John Campbell Shairp, *Sketches in History and Poetry* (Edinburgh, 1887), p. 342). ' "Kilmeny" s a well-known fairy piece' (David Daiches, *A Critical History of English Literature* (London, 1963), p. 830).

This seems quite unequivocal; and it should be added that the land of spirits is never called fairyland in the poem, nor are its inhabitants ever called fairies. In fact, they are very different beings from the fairies of another poem in *The Queen's Wake*—'Old David'. Here fairies are malevolent beings who pay tithes to the Devil, as in the old ballads. The spirits of 'Kilmeny', on the other hand, are 'meek and reverend', and they live in 'a land of love, and a land of light', from which they watch anxiously over the world, and 'grieve for the guilt of humanitye'. Further support for the view that the spirit-land of the poem is heaven is given by the linking narrative of the Wake, in which the bard who sings of Kilmeny is presented as a religious mystic. Hogg writes of him 'well versed was he in holy lore', and the following description is given of his home:

> Religion, man's first friend and best,
> Was in that home a constant guest.

There is overwhelming evidence, then, that 'Kilmeny' Is a religious poem, dealing with heaven, not fairyland. The only support for the view of the critics is a footnote by Hogg on the sources of the poem in popular traditions, in which he says that Kilmeny is taken to fairyland.[1] But surely this footnote cannot cancel out the unequivocal evidence of the poem itself.

If we accept the statement in the poem that the land to which Kilmeny is taken is heaven, then the events of the poem take on a new significance. In the opening lines Hogg tells of the mysterious disappearance of the beautiful Kilmeny, and of her return after an absence of seven years. He then turns to her adventures during that time. First of

[1] See Hogg's note to 'The Witch of Fife'. It is of course obvious that the story of Kilmeny is based on Border fairy legends of the kind to be found in ballads like 'Thomas the Rhymer' and 'Tam Lin'. Hogg, however, used these legends simply as a starting-point, and in 'Kilmeny' created a myth entirely different in its significance.

all she is received with rejoicing into the land of spirits, to which she has been taken because of her perfect purity—a purity so complete that it sets her far above all other women. She is then washed in the stream of life; and finally she is taken to a green mountain, where she is shown a vision of a lion and an eagle. The poem ends with a description of her brief return to earthly life.

In this myth Hogg articulates a deeply Christian view of the human situation; we live in a world of sin and sorrow, but behind and beyond our misery, at the transcendent level of experience, there is a joy which is eternal. In the words of the theologian Paul Tillich: 'The end of the way is joy. And joy is deeper than suffering. It is ultimate.'[1] In the words of the poem:

> But she saw till the sorrows of man were bye,
> And all was love and harmony;
> Till the stars of heaven fell calmly away,
> Like the flakes of snaw on a winter day.

The poem is an expression of the beauty and peace of that ultimate joy, seen against a background of the sadness of the contrast between the glory of heaven and our present situation.

Hogg enacts his vision superbly, especially in the great closing scene, in which Kilmeny returns to this world bringing some of the glory of heaven with her. She walks in the woodlands to sing her lonely hymns, and

> The wild beasts of the forest came,
> Broke from their bughts and faulds the tame . . .
> The blackbird alang wi' the eagle flew;
> The hind came tripping o'er the dew;
> The wolf and the kid their raike began
> And the tod, and the lamb, and the leveret ran . . .
> And all in a peaceful ring were hurled:
> It was like an eve in a sinless world!

[1] Paul Tillich, *The Shaking of the Foundations* (Harmondsworth, 1962), p. 69.

This is the joy of which Tillich speaks; this is the love and harmony we can expect when the stars of heaven fall calmly away. Hogg seems to echo Isaiah's vision of the New Jerusalem—'For, behold, I create new heavens and a new earth: and the former shall not be remembered, nor come into mind. But be ye glad and rejoice for ever *in that* which I create: for, behold, I create Jerusalem a rejoicing, and her people a joy . . . The wolf and the lamb shall feed together, and the lion shall eat straw like the bullock: and dust *shall be* the serpent's meat. They shall not hurt nor destroy in all my holy mountain, saith the Lord.'[1]

The joy and rejoicing of the new heavens and the new earth are even more amply conveyed in the opening sections of the poem, in which the glory of heaven is reflected in the quiet peace of the twilight in which Kilmeny returns, and in the awed wonder of her friends at her strange and holy calm. This first section of 'Kilmeny' is one of the most beautiful passages in Scottish literature.

The joy of the New Jerusalem is seen, as I have said, against a background of the sin and sorrow of the world. There is no easy way to it; it cannot be realized while the stars of heaven remain in their places. This is conveyed, in terms of the myth, by the fact that Kilmeny cannot remain in this world after her return. The poem ends thus:

> It wasna her hame, and she couldna remain;
> She left this world of sorrow and pain,
> And returned to the land of thought again.

This aspect of the poem's philosophy is made explicit in the choric comments of the spirits as they welcome Kilmeny into heaven. They praise her perfect purity, and contrast it with the general state of sin and sorrow of the world over which they watch.

This brings us to the least successful part of the poem, the scenes in heaven. Hogg's failure here is not really

[1] Isaiah 65: 17–18, 25. Compare also Isaiah 11: 6, 8–9.

surprising. The human mind cannot conceive heaven adequately, and any attempt to describe it directly is bound to end in anticlimax. We can perceive something of its nature only indirectly, through echoes and reflections, as in the opening and closing scenes of the poem. Nevertheless, although the scenes in heaven are inadequate and vaguely imagined, they do add something to the total significance of the myth. The bathing of Kilmeny in the stream of life helps to emphasise her semi-divine character, and the choric function of her reception into heaven has already been mentioned. The vision of the lion and the eagle remains to be considered. In this part of the poem, the spirits show Kilmeny the future up to the point where 'all was love and harmony'. Thus, by means of the vision, Hogg shows the reader that he has glimpsed something of the ultimate destiny of man in the love and harmony which Kilmeny's presence creates on her return to earth.

The vision also gives Hogg a chance to show the reader something of the sin and sorrow of the world, but unfortunately he only produces a superficial and somewhat chauvinistic account of the terrors of the French Revolution, and a pageant of the life of Mary Queen of Scots. In spite of these digressions, however, Hogg does convey in 'Kilmeny' something of the ultimate peace and joy which Christianity promises, something of the state of things when, in the words of St. Paul, 'that which is perfect is come'. This is an achievement of a very high order, an achievement worthy of the author of that great and profoundly disturbing novel, *The Private Memoirs and Confessions of a Justified Sinner*. It is the achievement of a poet of considerable importance.

CHRONOLOGY OF JAMES HOGG

Age

1770 (Nov.?) H. born at Ettrickhall farm in Ettrick Forest, the second of the four sons of Robert Hogg, a tenant-farmer, and his wife Margaret (*née* Laidlaw).

1777 Robert Hogg bankrupt. H. had to leave school, which he attended for only a few months in all. Remainder of his childhood spent in farm service, often in conditions of physical hardship.   6

1788 H. graduated from more menial work to become a shepherd in the service of Mr. Laidlaw of Willenslea. Here he was encouraged to read and to practise writing, an art he had almost forgotten.   17

1790–1800 H. employed as shepherd by a distant relative of his mother's, Mr. Laidlaw of Blackhouse in Yarrow. Here H. formed a close friendship with his employer's son William, later Scott's amanuensis. At Blackhouse H. used his employer's excellent library freely; he began to write verse, encouraged by William Laidlaw; and made his first publication—a poem contributed to *The Scots Magazine* in 1794.   19–29

1800 H.'s. war-song, 'Donald MacDonald', became popular throughout Scotland. He left Blackhouse to manage Ettrickhouse farm for his elderly parents.   29

1801 H. published a small volume of poems, *Scottish Pastorals*, which attracted little attention.   30

1802 H. met Scott, as a result of Scott's researches for vol. 3 of the *Border Minstrelsy*. H. had previously collected ballads for William Laidlaw to send to Scott. This meeting with Scott resulted in a lifelong friendship.   31

1803–7 H. prepared to move with his parents to a sheep-farm in Harris, but was refused possession of the farm because of a legal complication, and lost all his savings.   32–6

Age

He then became a shepherd in Nithsdale. During this period he made frequent contributions to *The Scots Magazine*.

1807 Scott persuaded Constable to publish H.'s *Mountain Bard* (poems attempting to improve on the ballad-imitations of the *Border Minstrelsy*) and his *Shepherd's Guide* (treatise on the diseases of sheep). H. earned £300 from these books. **36**

1807–10 H. lost all his money in unsuccessful farming ventures in Dumfriesshire. Returned to Ettrick in an unsuccessful attempt to find employment as a shepherd. **36–9**

1810 H. went to Edinburgh to become a professional writer. Published *The Forest Minstrel*, a collection of songs. **39**

1810–14 H. editor and main contributor of *The Spy*, a literary weekly journal which ran for a year. He was still in serious financial difficulties, but was given much help by two friends, John Grieve and Henry Scott. He also obtained some work as a land valuer, and he spoke regularly at The Forum, a debating club which attracted large public audiences. **39–43**

1813–15 *The Queen's Wake* was published in 1813, and H. became famous overnight. His financial problems remained as the publisher, Goldie, was bankrupt by 1814. Blackwood became the publisher of the poem, thus beginning a long association with H. The success of *The Queen's Wake* led to meetings with Wordsworth, De Quincey, Southey, and other leading men of letters. In 1815 H. was given Altrive Lake farm in Yarrow, rent-free and for life, by the Duke of Buccleuch. **42–4**

1817 *Blackwood's Magazine* founded. H. wrote the first draft of the famous 'Chaldee Manuscript', which scandalized Edinburgh and greatly increased *Blackwood's* readership. H. made frequent contributions to several periodicals from this time on. After this year H. turned increasingly to prose rather than poetry, a number of his poems having failed to gain success with the public. **46**

1818 H.'s novel *The Brownie of Bodsbeck* published. **47**

Age

1820   H. married Margaret Phillips (aged 31), whom he had   49
known for ten years. The marriage was a very happy
one, and five children were born to H. and his wife.

1821   H. took a nine-year lease of Mount Benger farm,   50
which was adjacent to Altrive Lake. He lost over two
thousands pounds at Mount Benger, which had already
ruined two competent farmers when he took it over.
On the expiry of the lease he returned to Altrive Lake.

1822   The first of the 'Noctes Ambrosianae' appeared in   51
Blackwood's. The series continued until H.'s death.

1824   The *Confessions of a Justified Sinner* published.   53

1825   'Queen Hynde', H.'s longest poem, which had been   54
begun and abandoned in 1817, was completed and
published. This poems shows H. at his worst.

1832   H. visited London to arrange the publication of a   61
collected edition of his prose, *Altrive Tales*. Cochrane,
the publisher, became bankrupt after the publication
of the first volume. H. stayed in London for three
months, and was lionized. In this year Scott died.

1834   H.'s *Familiar Anecdotes of Sir Walter Scott* published   63
in New York, and later in Britain as *The Domestic
Manners and Private Life of Sir Walter Scott*.

1835   H. prepared a fresh prose collection—*Tales of the   64
Wars of Montrose*—for publication. Cochrane, who
had resumed business, was again the publisher, but
was bankrupt within a few months. At the end of
October H. became seriously ill, and in November he
died.

THE QUEEN'S WAKE

INTRODUCTION

Now burst, ye Winter clouds that lower,
Fling from your folds the piercing shower;
Sing to the tower and leafless tree,
Ye cold winds of adversity;
Your blights, your chilling influence shed,   5
On wareless heart, and houseless head,
Your ruth or fury I disdain,
I've found my Mountain Lyre again.

  Come to my heart, my only stay!
Companion of a happier day!   10
Thou gift of Heaven, thou pledge of good,
Harp of the mountain and the wood!
I little thought, when first I tried
Thy notes by lone Saint Mary's side,
When in a deep untrodden den,   15
I found thee in the braken glen,
I little thought that idle toy
Should e'er become my only joy!

  A maiden's youthful smiles had wove
Around my heart the toils of love,   20
When first thy magic wires I rung,
And on the breeze thy numbers flung.
The fervid tear played in mine eye;
I trembled, wept, and wondered why.

Sweet was the thrilling ecstacy: 25
I know not if 'twas love or thee.

Weened not my heart, when youth had flown
Friendship would fade, or fortune frown;
When pleasure, love, and mirth were past,
That thou should'st prove my all at last!   30
Jeered by conceit and lordly pride,
I flung my soothing harp aside;
With wayward fortune strove a while;
Wrecked in a world of self and guile.
Again I sought the braken hill;   35
Again sat musing by the rill;
My wild sensations all were gone,
And only thou wert left alone.
Long hast thou in the moorland lain,
Now welcome to my heart again.   40

The russet weed of mountain gray
No more shall round thy border play;
No more the brake-flowers, o'er thee piled,
Shall mar thy tones and measures wild.
Harp of the Forest, thou shalt be   45
Fair as the bud on forest tree!
Sweet be thy strains, as those that swell
In Ettrick's green and fairy dell;
Soft as the breeze of falling even,
And purer than the dews of heaven.   50

Of minstrel honours, now no more;
Of bards, who sung in days of yore;
Of gallant chiefs, in courtly guise;
Of ladies' smiles, of ladies' eyes;
O f royal feast and obsequies;   55

When Caledon, with look severe,
Saw Beauty's hand her sceptre bear,—
By cliff and haunted wild I'll sing,
Responsive to thy dulcet string.

When wanes the circling year away, 60
When scarcely smiles the doubtful day,
Fair daughter of Dunedin, say,
Hast thou not heard, at midnight deep,
Soft music on thy slumbers creep?
At such a time, if careless thrown 65
Thy slender form on couch of down,
Hast thou not felt, to nature true,
The tear steal from thine eye so blue?
If then thy guiltless bosom strove
In blissful dreams of conscious love, 70
And even shrunk from proffer bland
Of lover's visionary hand,
On such ecstatic dream when brake
The music of the midnight Wake,
Hast thou not weened thyself on high, 75
List'ning to angels' melody,
'Scaped from a world of cares away,
To dream of love and bliss for aye?

The dream dispelled, the music gone,
Hast thou not, sighing, all alone, 80
Proffered thy vows to Heaven, and then
Blest the sweet Wake, and slept again?

Then list, ye maidens, to my lay,
Though old the tale, and past the day;
Those Wakes, now played by minstrels poor, 85
At midnight's darkest, chillest hour

Those humble Wakes, now scorned by all,
Were first begun in courtly hall,
When royal MARY, blithe of mood,
Kept holiday at Holyrood.   90

    Scotland, involved in factious broils,
Groaned deep beneath her woes and toils,
And looked o'er meadow, dale, and lea,
For many a day her Queen to see;
Hoping that then her woes would cease,   95
And all her vallies smile in peace.
The Spring was past, the Summer gone;
Still vacant stood the Scottish throne:
But scarce had Autumn's mellow hand
Waved her rich banner o'er the land,   100
When rang the shouts, from tower and tree,
That Scotland's Queen was on the sea.
Swift spread the news o'er down and dale,
Swift as the lively autumn gale;
Away, away, it echoed still,   105
O'er many a moor and Highland hill,
Till rang each glen and verdant plain,
From Cheviot to the northern main.

    Each bard attuned the loyal lay,
And for Dunedin hied away;   110
Each harp was strung in woodland bower,
In praise of beauty's bonniest flower.
The chiefs forsook their ladies fair;
The priest his beads and books of prayer;
The farmer left his harvest day,   115
The shepherd all his flocks to stray;
The forester forsook the wood,
And hasted on to Holyrood.

After a youth, by woes o'ercast,
After a thousand sorrows past,   120
The lovely Mary once again
Set foot upon her native plain;
Kneeled on the pier with modest grace,
And turned to heaven her beauteous face.
'Twas then the caps in air were blended,   125
A thousand thousand shouts ascended;
Shivered the breeze around the throng;
Gray barrier cliffs the peals prolong;
And every tongue gave thanks to Heaven,
That Mary to their hopes was given.   130

Her comely form and graceful mien,
Bespoke the Lady and the Queen;
The woes of one so fair and young,
Moved every heart and every tongue.
Driven from her home, a helpless child,   135
To brave the winds and billows wild;
An exile bred in realms afar,
Amid commotion, broil, and war.
In one short year her hopes all crossed,—
A parent, husband, kingdom lost!   140
And all ere eighteen years had shed
Their honours o'er her royal head.
For such a Queen, the Stuarts' heir,
A Queen so courteous, young, and fair,
Who would not every foe defy!   145
Who would not stand! who would not die!

Light on her airy steed she sprung,
Around with golden tassels hung,
No chieftain there rode half so free,
Or half so light and gracefully.   150

How sweet to see her ringlets pale
Wide waving in the southland gale,
Which through the broom-wood blossoms flew,
To fan her cheeks of rosy hue!
Whene'er it heaved her bosom's screen,   155
What beauties in her form were seen!
And when her courser's mane it swung,
A thousand silver bells were rung.
A sight so fair, on Scottish plain,
A Scot shall never see again.   160

   When **Mary** turned her wondering eyes
On rocks that seemed to prop the skies;
On palace, park, and battled pile;
On lake, on river, sea, and isle;
O'er woods and meadows bathed in dew,   165
To distant mountains wild and blue;
She thought the isle that gave her birth,
The sweetest, wildest land on earth.

   Slowly she ambled on her way
Amid her lords and ladies gay.   170
Priest, abbot, layman, all were there,
And Presbyter with look severe.
There rode the lords of France and Spain,
Of England, Flanders, and Lorraine,
While serried thousands round them stood,   175
From shore of Leith to Holyrood.

   Though Mary's heart was light as air
To find a home so wild and fair;
To see a gathered nation by,
And rays of joy from every eye;   180

Though frequent shouts the welkin broke,
Though courtiers bowed and ladies spoke,
An absent look they oft could trace
Deep settled on her comely face.
Was it the thought, that all alone   185
She must support a rocking throne?
That Caledonia's rugged land
Might scorn a Lady's weak command,
And the Red Lion's haughty eye
Scowl at a maiden's feet to lie?   190

  No; 'twas the notes of Scottish song,
Soft pealing from the countless throng.
So mellowed came the distant swell,
That on her ravished ear it fell
Like dew of heaven, at evening close,   195
On forest flower or woodland rose.
For Mary's heart, to nature true,
The powers of song and music knew:
But all the choral measures bland,
Of anthems sung in southern land,   200
Appeared an useless pile of art,
Unfit to sway or melt the heart,
Compared with that which floated by,—
Her simple native melody.

  As she drew nigh the Abbey stile,   205
She halted, reined, and bent the while:
She heard the Caledonian lyre
Pour forth its notes of runic fire;
But scarcely caught the ravished Queen,
The minstrel's song that flowed between;   210
Entranced upon the strain she hung,
'Twas thus the gray-haired minstrel sung.—

The Song

"O! Lady dear, fair is thy noon,
But man is like the inconstant moon:
Last night she smiled o'er lawn and lea;   215
That moon will change, and so will he.

"Thy time, dear Lady, 's a passing shower;
Thy beauty is but a fading flower;
Watch thy young bosom, and maiden eye,
For the shower must fall, and the flow'ret die."— 220

What ails my Queen? said good Argyle,
Why fades upon her cheek the smile?
Say, rears your steed too fierce and high?
Or sits your golden seat awry?

Ah! no, my Lord! this noble steed,   225
Of Rouen's calm and generous breed,
Has borne me over hill and plain,
Swift as the dun-deer of the Seine.
But such a wild and simple lay,
Poured from the harp of minstrel gray,   230
My every sense away it stole,
And swayed a while my raptured soul.
O! say, my Lord (for you must know
What strains along your vallies flow,
And all the hoards of Highland lore),   235
Was ever song so sweet before?—

Replied the Earl, as round he flung,—
Feeble the strain that minstrel sung!
My royal Dame, if once you heard
The Scottish lay from Highland bard,   240
Then might you say, in raptures meet,
No song was ever half so sweet!

It nerves the arm of warrior wight
To deeds of more than mortal might;
'Twill make the maid, in all her charms,   245
Fall weeping in her lover's arms;
'Twill charm the mermaid from the deep;
Make mountain oaks to bend and weep;
Thrill every heart with horrors dire,
And shape the breeze to forms of fire.   250

When poured from greenwood-bower at even,
'Twill draw the spirits down from heaven;
And all the fays that haunt the wood,
To dance around in frantic mood,
And tune their mimic harps so boon   255
Beneath the cliff and midnight moon.
Ah! yes, my Queen! if once you heard
The Scottish lay from Highland bard,
Then might you say in raptures meet,
No song was ever half so sweet.—   260

Queen Mary lighted in the court;
Queen Mary joined the evening's sport;
Yet though at table all were seen,
To wonder at her air and mien;
Though courtiers fawned and ladies sung,   265
Still in her ear the accents rung,—
"*Watch thy young bosom, and maiden eye,*
"*For the shower must fall, and the flowret die.*"
These words prophetic seemed to be,
Foreboding wo and misery;   270
And much she wished to prove ere long,
The wonderous powers of Scottish song.

When next to ride the Queen was bound,
To view the city's ample round,

On high amid the gathered crowd, 275
A herald thus proclaim'd aloud:—

"Peace, peace to Scotland's wasted vales,
To her dark heaths and Highland dales;
To her brave sons of warlike mood,
To all her daughters fair and good; 280
Peace o'er her ruined vales shall pour,
Like beam of heaven behind the shower.
Let every harp and echo ring;
Let maidens smile and poets sing;
For love and peace entwined shall sleep, 285
Calm as the moon-beam on the deep;
By waving wood and wandering rill,
On purple heath and Highland hill.

"The soul of warrior stern to charm,
And bigotry and rage disarm, 290
Our Queen commands, that every bard
Due honours have, and high regard.
If, to his song of rolling fire,
He join the Caledonian lyre,
And skill in legendary lore, 295
Still higher shall his honours soar.
For all the arts beneath the heaven,
That man has found, or God has given,
None draws the soul so sweet away,
As music's melting mystic lay; 300
Slight emblem of the bliss above,
It sooths the spirit all to love.

"To cherish this attractive art,
To lull the passions, mend the heart,

And break the moping zealot's chains, 305
Hear what our lovely Queen ordains.

"Each Caledonian bard must seek
Her courtly halls on Christmas week,
That then the Royal Wake may be
Cheered by their thrilling minstrelsy. 310
No ribaldry the Queen must hear,
No song unmeet for maiden's ear,
No jest, nor adulation bland,
But legends of our native land;
And he whom most the court regards, 315
High be his honours and rewards.
Let every Scottish bard give ear,
Let every Scottish bard appear;
He then before the court must stand,
In native garb, with harp in hand. 320
At home no minstrel dare to tarry:
High the behest.—God save Queen Mary!"

Little recked they, that idle throng,
O music's power or minstrel's song;
But crowding their young Queen around, 325
Whose stately courser pawed the ground,
Her beauty more their wonder swayed,
Than all the noisy herald said;
Judging the proffer all in sport,
An idle whim of idle court. 330
But many a bard preferred his prayer;
For many a Scottish bard was there.
Quaked each fond heart with raptures strong,
Each thought upon his harp and song;
And turning home without delay, 335
Coned his wild strain by mountain gray.

Each glen was sought for tales of old,
Of luckless love, of warrior bold,
Of ravished maid, or stolen child
By freakish fairy of the wild;   340
Of sheeted ghost, that had revealed
Dark deeds of guilt from man concealed;
Of boding dreams, of wandering spright,
Of dead-lights glimmering through the night;
Yea, every tale of ruth or weir,   345
Could waken pity, love, or fear,
Were decked anew, with anxious pain,
And sung to native airs again.

Alas! those lays of fire once more
Are wrecked 'mid heaps of mouldering lore!   350
And feeble he who dares presume
That heavenly Wake-light to relume.
But, grieved the legendary lay
Should perish from our land for aye,
While sings the lark above the wold,   355
And all his flocks rest in the fold,
Fondly he strikes, beside the pen,
The harp of Yarrow's braken glen.

December came; his aspect stern
Glared deadly o'er the mountain cairn;   360
A polar sheet was round him flung,
And ice-spears at his girdle hung;
O'er frigid field, and drifted cone,
He strode undaunted and alone;
Or, throned amid the Grampians gray,   365
Kept thaws and suns of heaven at bay.

Not stern December's fierce control
Could quench the flame of minstrel's soul:

Little recked they, our bards of old,
Of Autumn's showers, or Winter's cold.   370
Sound slept they on the nighted hill,
Lulled by the winds or babbling rill:
Curtained within the Winter cloud,
The heath their couch, the sky their shroud.
Yet their's the strains that touch the heart,   375
Bold, rapid, wild, and void of art.

Unlike the bards, whose milky lays
Delight in these degenerate days:
Their crystal spring, and heather brown,
Is changed to wine and couch of down;   380
Effeminate as lady gay,—
Such as the bard, so is his lay!

But then was seen, from every vale,
Through drifting snows and rattling hail,
Each Caledonian minstrel true,   385
Dressed in his plaid and bonnet blue,
With harp across his shoulders slung,
And music murmuring round his tongue,
Forcing his way, in raptures high,
To Holyrood his skill to try.   390

Ah! when at home the songs they raised,
When gaping rustics stood and gazed,
Each bard believed, with ready will,
Unmatched his song, unmatched his skill!
But when the royal halls appeared,   395
Each aspect changed, each bosom feared;
And when in court of Holyrood
Filed harps and bards around him stood,

His eye emitted cheerless ray,
His hope, his spirit sunk away: 400
There stood the minstrel, but his mind
Seemed left in native glen behind.

Unknown to men of sordid heart,
What joys the poet's hopes impart;
Unknown, how his high soul is torn   405
By cold neglect, or canting scorn:
That meteor torch of mental light,
A breath can quench, or kindle bright.
Oft has that mind, which braved serene
The shafts of poverty and pain,   410
The Summer toil, the Winter blast,
Fallen victim to a frown at last.
Easy the boon he asks of thee;
O! spare his heart in courtesy!

There rolled each bard his anxious eye,   415
Or strode his adversary by.
No cause was there for names to scan,
Each minstrel's plaid bespoke his clan;
And the blunt borderer's plain array,
The bonnet broad and blanket gray.   420
Bard sought of bard a look to steal;
Eyes measured each from head to heel.
Much wonder rose, that men so famed,
Men save with rapture never named,
Looked only so,—they could not tell,—   425
Like other men, and scarce so well.
Though keen the blast, and long the way,
When twilight closed that dubious day,
When round the table all were set,
Small heart had they to talk or eat;   430

Red look askance, blunt whisper low,
Awkward remark, uncourtly bow,
Were all that past in that bright throng,
That group of genuine sons of song.

One did the honours of the board,   435
Who seemed a courtier or a lord.
Strange his array and speech withal,
Gael deemed him southern—southern, Gael.
Courteous his mien, his accents weak,
Lady in manner as in make;   440
Yet round the board a whisper ran,
That that same gay and simpering man
A minstrel was of wonderous fame,
Who from a distant region came,
To bear the prize beyond the sea   445
To the green shores of Italy.

The wine was served, and, sooth to say,
Insensibly it stole away.
Thrice did they drain the allotted store,
And wondering skinkers dun for more;   450
Which vanished swifter than the first,—
Little weened they the poets' thirst.

Still as that ruddy juice they drained,
The eyes were cleared, the speech regained;
And latent sparks of fancy glowed,   455
Till one abundant torrent flowed
Of wit, of humour, social glee,
Wild music, mirth, and revelry.

Just when a jest had thrilled the crowd,
Just when the laugh was long and loud,   460

Entered a squire with summons smart;—
That was the knell that pierced the heart!— ·
"The court awaits;" he bowed—was gone,—
Our bards sat changed to busts of stone.
As ever ye heard the green-wood dell,　　　465
On morn of June one warbled swell,
If burst the thunder from on high,
How hushed the woodland melody!
Even so our bards shrunk at the view
Of what they wished, and what they knew.　　　470

　　Their numbers given, the lots were cast,
To fix the names of first and last;
Then to the dazzling hall were led,
Poor minstrels less alive than dead.

　　There such a scene entranced the view,　　　475
As heart of poet never knew.
'Twas not the flash of golden gear,
Nor blaze of silver chandelier;
Not Scotland's chiefs of noble air,
Nor dazzling rows of ladies fair;　　　480
'Twas one enthroned the rest above,—
Sure 'twas the Queen of grace and love!
Taper the form, and fair the breast
Yon radiant golden zones invest,
Where the vexed rubies blench in death,　　　485
Beneath yon lips and balmy breath.
Coronel gems of every dye,
Look dim above yon beaming eye:
Yon cheeks outvie the dawning's glow,
Red shadowed on a wreath of snow.　　　490

　　Oft the rapt bard had thought alone,
Of charms by mankind never known,

Of virgins, pure as opening day,
Or bosom of the flower of May:
Oft dreamed of beings free from stain, 495
Of maidens of the emerald main,
Of fairy dames in grove at even,
Of angels in the walks of heaven:
But, nor in earth, the sea, nor sky,
In fairy dream, nor fancy's eye, 500
Vision his soul had ever seen
Like MARY STUART, Scotland's Queen.

———

FROM NIGHT THE FIRST

[THE EIGHTH BARD]

THE eighth was from the Leven coast:
The rest who sung that night are lost.

Mounted the bard of Fife on high,
Bushy his beard, and wild his eye:
His cheek was furrowed by the gale, [5]
And his thin locks were long and pale.
Full hardly passed he through the throng,
Dragging on crutches, slow along,
His feeble and unhealthy frame,
And kindness welcomed as he came. [10]
His unpresuming aspect mild,
Calm and benignant as a child,
Yet spoke to all that viewed him nigh,
That more was there than met the eye.
Some wizard of the shore he seemed, [15]
Who through the scenes of life had dreamed,

Of spells that vital life benumb,
Of formless spirits wandering dumb,
Where aspins in the moon-beam quake,
By mouldering pile, or mountain lake.   [20]

He deemed that fays and spectres wan
Held converse with the thoughts of man;
In dreams their future fates foretold,
And spread the death-flame on the wold;
Or flagged at eve each restless wing,   [25]
In dells their vesper hymns to sing.

Such was our bard, such were his lays:
And long by green Benarty's base,
His wild wood notes, from ivy cave,
Had waked the dawning from the wave.   [30]
At evening fall, in lonesome dale,
He kept strange converse with the gale;
Held worldly pomp in high derision,
And wandered in a world of vision.

Of mountain ash his harp was framed,   [35]
The brazen chords all trembling flamed,
As in a rugged northern tongue,
This mad unearthly song he sung.

The Witch of Fife

THE EIGHTH BARD'S SONG

"Quhare haif ye been, ye ill womyne,
    These three lang nightis fra hame?
Quhat garris the sweit drap fra yer brow,
    Like clotis of the saut sea faem?

"It fearis me muckil ye haif seen   5
   Quhat good man never knew;
It fearis me muckil ye haif been
   Quhare the gray cock never crew.

"But the spell may crack, and the brydel breck,
   Then sherpe yer werde will be;   10
Ye had better sleipe in yer bed at hame,
   Wi' yer deire littil bairnis and me."—

'Sit dune, sit dune, my leil auld man,
   Sit dune, and listin to me;
I'll gar the hayre stand on yer crown,   15
   And the cauld sweit blind yer e'e.

'But tell nae wordis, my gude auld man,
   Tell never word again;
Or deire shall be yer courtisye,
   And driche and sair yer pain.   20

'The first leet night, quhan the new moon set,
   Quhan all was douffe and mirk,
We saddled ouir naigis wi' the moon-fern leif,
   And rode fra Kilmerrin kirk.

'Some horses ware of the brume-cow framit,   25
   And some of the greine bay tree;
But mine was made of ane humloke schaw,
   And a stout stallion was he.

'We raide the tod doune on the hill,
   The martin on the law;   30
And we huntyd the hoolet out of brethe,
   And forcit him doune to fa.'—

"Quhat guid was that, ye ill womyne?
　　Quhat guid was that to thee?
Ye wald better haif been in yer bed at hame,   35
　　Wi' yer deire littil bairnis and me."—

'And aye we raide, and se merrily we raide,
　　Throw the merkist gloffis of the night;
And we swam the floode, and we darnit the woode,
　　Till we cam to the Lommond height.   40

'And quhen we cam to the Lommond height,
　　Se lythlye we lychtid doune;
And we drank fra the hornis that never grew,
　　The beer that was never browin.

'Then up there raise ane wee wee man,   45
　　Franethe the moss-gray stane;
His fece was wan like the collifloure,
　　For he nouthir had blude nor bane.

'He set ane reid-pipe till his muthe,
　　And he playit se bonnilye,   50
Till the gray curlew, and the black-cock, flew
　　To listen his melodye.

'It rang se sweet through the grein Lommond,
　　That the nycht-winde lowner blew;
And it soupit alang the Loch Leven,   55
　　And wakinit the white sea-mew.

'It rang se sweet through the grein Lommond,
　　Se sweitly butt and se shill,
That the wezilis laup out of their mouldy holis,
　　And dancit on the mydnycht hill.   60

'The corby craw cam gledgin near,
   The ern gede veeryng bye;
And the troutis laup out of the Leven Loch,
   Charmit with the melodye.

'And aye we dancit on the grein Lommond,   65
   Till the dawn on the ocean grew:
Ne wonder I was a weary wycht
   Quhan I cam hame to you.'—

"Quhat guid, quhat guid, my weird weird wyfe,
   Quhat guid was that to thee?   70
Ye wald better haif bein in yer bed at hame,
   Wi' yer deire littil bairnis and me."

'The second nycht, quhan the new moon set,
   O'er the roaryng sea we flew;
The cockle-shell our trusty bark,   75
   Our sailis of the grein sea-rue.

'And the bauld windis blew, and the fire-flauchtis flew,
   And the sea ran to the skie;
And the thunner it growlit, and the sea-dogs howlit,
   As we gaed scouryng bye.   80

'And aye we mountit the sea-green hillis,
   Quhill we brushit thro' the cludis of the hevin;
Than sousit dounright like the stern-shot light,
   Fra the liftis blue casement driven.

'But our taickil stood, and our bark was good,   85
   And se pang was our pearily prowe;
Quhan we culdna speil the brow of the wavis,
   We needilit them throu belowe.

'As fast as the hail, as fast as the gale,
    As fast as the midnycht leme,   90
We borit the breiste of the burstyng swale,
    Or fluffit i' the flotyng faem.

'And quhan to the Norraway shore we wan,
    We muntyd our steedis of the wynd,
And we splashit the floode, and we darnit the woode,
    And we left the shouir behynde.   96

'Fleet is the roe on the grein Lommond,
    And swift is the couryng grew;
The rein-deer dun can eithly run,
    Quhan the houndis and the hornis pursue.   100

'But nowther the roe, nor the rein-deer dun,
    The hinde nor the couryng grew,
Culd fly owr muntaine, muir, and dale,
    As owr braw steedis they flew.

'The dales war deep, and the Doffrinis steep,   105
    And we rase to the skyis e'e-bree;
Quhite, quhite was ouir rode, that was never trode,
    Owr the snawis of eternity!

'And quhan we cam to the Lapland lone,
    The fairies war all in array;   110
For all the genii of the north
    War keepyng their holeday.

'The warlock men and the weird wemyng,
    And the fays of the wood and the steep,
And the phantom hunteris all war there,   115
    And the mermaidis of the deep.

'And they washit us all with the witch-water,
   Distillit fra the moorland dew,
Quhill our beauty blumit like the Lapland rose,
   That wylde in the foreste grew.'—   120

"Ye lee, ye lee, ye ill womyne,
   Se loud as I heir ye lee!
For the warst-faurd wyfe on the shoris of Fyfe
   Is cumlye comparet wi' thee."—

'Then the mer-maidis sang and the woodlandis rang, 125
   Se sweetly swellit the quire;
On every cliff a herpe they hang,
   On every tree a lyre.

'And aye they sang, and the woodlandis rang,
   And we drank, and we drank se deep;   130
Then soft in the armis of the warlock men,
   We laid us dune to sleep.'—

"Away, away, ye ill womyne,
   An ill deide met ye dee!
Quhan ye hae pruvit se false to yer God,   135
   Ye can never pruve trew to me."—

'And there we lernit fra the fairy foke,
   And fra our master true,
The wordis that can beire us throu the air,
   And lokkis and baris undo. —   140

'Last nycht we met at Maisry's cot;
   Richt weil the wordis we knew;
And we set a foot on the black cruik-shell,
   And out at the lum we flew.

'And we flew owr hill, and we flew owr dale,   145
    And we flew owr firth and sea,
Until we cam to merry Carlisle,
    Quhar we lightit on the lea.

'We gaed to the vault beyound the towir,
    Quhar we enterit free as ayr;   150
And we drank, and we drank of the bishopis wine
    Quhill we culde drynk ne mair.'—

"Gin that be trew, my gude auld wyfe,
    Whilk thou hast tauld to me,
Betide my death, betide my lyfe,   155
    I'll beire thee companye.

"Neist tyme ye gaung to merry Carlisle
    To drynk of the blude-reid wine,
Beshrew my heart, I'll fly with thee,
    If the diel should fly behynde."   160

'Ah! little do ye ken, my silly auld man,
    The daingeris we maun dree;
Last nichte we drank of the bishopis wyne,
    Quhill near near taen war we.

'Afore we wan to the sandy ford,   165
    The gor-cockis nichering flew;
The lofty crest of Ettrick Pen
    Was wavit about with blew,
And, flichtering throu the air, we fand
    The chill chill mornyng dew.   170

'As we flew owr the hillis of Braid,
    The sun rase fair and clear;
There gurly James, and his baronis braw,
    War out to hunt the deere.

'Their bowis they drew, their arrowis flew,   175
    And peircit the ayr with speede,
Quhill purpil fell the mornyng dew
    With witch-blude rank and reide.

'Littil do ye ken, my silly auld man,
    The dangeris we maun dree;   180
Ne wonder I am a weary wycht
    Quhan I come hame to thee.'—

"But tell me the *word*, my gude auld wyfe,
    Come tell it me speedilye:
For I lang to drink of the gude reide wyne,   185
    And to wyng the ayr with thee.

"Yer hellish horse I wilna ryde,
    Nor sail the seas in the wynd;
But I can flee as well as thee,
    And I'll drynk quhile ye be blynd."—   190

'O fy! O fy! my leil auld man,
    That word I darena tell;
It wald turn this warld all upside down,
    And make it warse than hell.

'For all the lasses in the land   195
    Wald munt the wynd and fly;
And the men wald doff their doublets syde,
    And after them wald ply.'—

But the auld gudeman was ane cunnyng auld man,
    And ane cunnyng auld man was he;   200
And he watchit, and he watchit for mony a nychte,
    The witches' flychte to see.

Ane nychte he darnit in Maisry's cot;
   The fearless haggs came in;
And he heard the word of awsome weird,   205
   And he saw their deedis of synn.

Then ane by ane, they said that word,
   As fast to the fire they drew;
Then set a foot on the black cruik-shell,
   And out at the lum they flew.   210

The auld gudeman cam fra his hole
   With feire and muckil dreide,
But yet he culdna think to rue,
   For the wyne came in his head.

He set his foot in the black cruik-shell,   215
   With ane fixit and ane wawlyng e'e;
And he said the word that I darena say,
   And out at the lum flew he.

The witches skalit the moon-beam pale;
   Deep groanit the trembling wynde;   220
But they never wist till our auld gudeman
   Was hoveryng them behynde.

They flew to the vaultis of merry Carlisle,
   Quhair they enterit free as ayr;
And they drank and they drank of the bishopis wyne
   Quhill they culde drynk ne mair.   226

The auld gudeman he grew se crouse,
   He dancit on the mouldy ground,
And he sang the bonniest sangs of Fife,
   And he tuzzlit the kerlyngs round.   230

And aye he peircit the tither butt,
    And he suckit, and he suckit se lang,
Quhill his e'en they closit, and his voice grew low,
    And his tongue wald hardly gang.

The kerlyngs drank of the bishopis wyne   235
    Quhill they scentit the mornyng wynde;
Then clove again the yeilding ayr,
    And left the auld man behynde.

And aye he slepit on the damp damp floor,
    He slepit and he snorit amain;   240
He never dreamit he was far fra hame,
    Or that the auld wyvis war gane.

And aye he slepit on the damp damp floor,
    Quhill past the mid-day highte,
Quhan wakenit by five rough Englishmen,   245
    That trailit him to the lychte.

"Now quha are ye, ye silly auld man,
    That sleepis se sound and se weil?
Or how gat ye into the bishopis vault
    Throu lokkis and barris of steel?"   250

The auld gudeman he tryit to speak,
    But ane word he culdna fynde;
He tryit to think, but his head whirlit round,
    And ane thing he culdna mynde:—
"I cam fra Fyfe," the auld man cryit,   255
    "And I cam on the midnight wynde."

They nickit the auld man, and they prickit the auld man,
    And they yerkit his limbis with twine,
Quhill the reide blude ran in his hose and shoon,
    But some cryit it was wyne.   260

They lickit the auld man, and they prickit the auld
    man,
    And they tyit him till ane stone;
And they set ane bele-fire him about,
    To burn him skin and bone.

"O wae to me!" said the puir auld man,   265
    "That ever I saw the day!
And wae be to all the ill wemyng
    That lead puir men astray!

"Let nevir ane auld man after this
    To lawless greide inclyne;   270
Let nevir ane auld man after this
    Rin post to the deil for wyne."

The reike flew up in the auld manis face,
    And choukit him bitterlye;
And the lowe cam up with ane angry blese,   275
    And it syngit his auld breek-nee.

He lukit to the land fra whence he came,
    For lukis he culde get ne mae;
And he thochte of his deire littil bairnis at hame,
    And O the auld man was wae!   280

But they tunrit their facis to the sun,
    With gloffe and wonderous glair,
For they saw ane thing beth lairge and dun,
    Comin swaipin down the aire.

That burd it cam fra the landis o' Fife,   285
    And it cam rycht tymeouslye,
For quha was it but the auld manis wife,
    Just comit his dethe to see.

Scho pat ane reide cap on his heide,
    And the auld gudeman lookit fain, 290
Then whisperit ane word intil his lug,
    And tovit to the aire again.

The auld gudeman he gae ane bob
    I' the mids o' the burnyng lowe;
And the sheklis that band him to the ring, 295
    They fell fra his armis like towe.

He drew his breath, and he said the word,
    And he said it with muckle glee,
Then set his fit on the burnyng pile,
    And away to the aire flew he. 300

Till aince he cleirit the swirlyng reike,
    He lukit beth ferit and sad;
But whan he wan to the lycht blue aire,
    He lauchit as he'd been mad.

His armis war spred, and his heide was hiche, 305
    And his feite stack out behynde;
And the laibies of the auld manis cote
    War wauffyng in the wynde.

And aye he neicherit, and aye he flew,
    For he thochte the ploy se raire; 310
It was like the voice of the gainder blue,
    Whan he flees throu the aire.

He lukit back to the Carlisle men
    As he borit the norlan sky;
He noddit his heide, and gae ane girn, 315
    But he nevir said gude-bye.

They vanisht far i' the liftis blue wale,
   Ne maire the English saw,
But the auld manis lauche cam on the gale,
   With a lang and a loud gaffa.   320

May everilke man in the land of Fife
   Read what the drinkeris dree;
And nevir curse his puir auld wife,
   Rychte wicked altho scho be.

━━━━━

FROM NIGHT THE SECOND

[THE THIRTEENTH BARD]

AGAIN is every courtier's gaze
Speaking suspense, and deep amaze;
The bard was stately, dark and stern,—
'Twas Drummond from the moors of Ern.
Tall was his frame, his forehead high,   [5]
Still and mysterious was his eye;
His look was like a winter day,
When storms and winds have sunk away.

Well versed was he in holy lore;
In cloistered dome the cowl he wore;   [10]
But, wearied with the eternal strain
Of formal breviats, cold and vain,
He wooed, in depth of Highland dale,
The silver spring and mountain gale.

In gray Glen-Ample's forest deep,   [15]
Hid from the rains and tempest's sweep,
In bosom of an aged wood
His solitary cottage stood.

Its walls were bastioned, dark, and dern,
Dark was its roof of filmot fern,   [20]
And dark the vista down the linn,
But all was love and peace within.
Religion, man's first friend and best,
Was in that home a constant guest;
There, sweetly, every morn and even,   [25]
Warm orisons were poured to Heaven:
And every cliff Glen-Ample knew,
And green wood on her banks that grew,
In answer to his bounding string,
Had learned the hymns of Heaven to sing;   [30]
With many a song of mystic lore,
Rude as when sung in days of yore.

   His were the snowy flocks, that strayed
Adown Glen-Airtney's forest glade;
And his the goat, and chesnut hind,   [35]
Where proud Ben-Vorlich cleaves the wind:
There oft, when suns of summer shone,
The bard would sit, and muse alone,
Of innocence, expelled by man;
Of nature's fair and wonderous plan;   [40]
Of the eternal throne sublime,
Of visions seen in ancient time,
Till his rapt soul would leave her home
In visionary worlds to roam.
Then would the mists that wandered bye   [45]
Seem hovering spirits to his eye:
Then would the breeze's whistling sweep,
Soft lulling in the cavern deep,
Seem to the enthusiast's dreaming ear
The words of spirits whispered near.   [50]

Loathed his firm soul the measured chime
And florid films of modern rhyme;
No other lays became his tongue
But those his rude forefathers sung.
And when, by wandering minstrel warned,   [55]
The mandate of his queen he learned,
So much he prized the ancient strain,
High hopes had he the prize to gain.
With modest, yet majestic mien,
He tuned his harp of solemn strain: [60]
O list the tale, ye fair and young,
A lay so strange was never sung!

Kilmeny

THE THIRTEENTH BARD'S SONG

Bonny Kilmeny gaed up the glen;
But it wasna to meet Duneira's men,
Nor the rosy monk of the isle to see,
For Kilmeny was pure as pure could be.
It was only to hear the Yorlin sing,   5
And pu' the cress-flower round the spring;
The scarlet hypp and the hindberrye,
And the nut that hang frae the hazel tree;
For Kilmeny was pure as pure could be.
But lang may her minny look o'er the wa',   10
And lang may she seek i' the green-wood shaw;
Lang the laird of Duneira blame,
And lang, lang greet or Kilmeny come hame!

When many a day had come and fled,
When grief grew calm, and hope was dead,   15

When mess for Kilmeny's soul had been sung,
When the bedes-man had prayed, and the dead-
      bell rung,
Late, late in a gloamin when all was still,
When the fringe was red on the westlin hill,
The wood was sere, the moon i' the wane,   20
The reek o' the cot hung over the plain,
Like a little wee cloud in the world its lane;
When the ingle lowed with an eiry leme,
Late, late in the gloamin Kilmeny came hame!

"Kilmeny, Kilmeny, where have you been?   25
Lang hae we sought baith holt and den;
By linn, by ford, and green-wood tree,
Yet you are halesome and fair to see.
Where gat you that joup o' the lilly scheen?
That bonny snood of the birk sae green?   30
And these roses, the fairest that ever were seen?
Kilmeny, Kilmeny, where have you been?"

Kilmeny looked up with a lovely grace,
But nae smile was seen on Kilmeny's face;
As still was her look, and as still was her ee,   35
As the stillness that lay on the emerant lea,
Or the mist that sleeps on a waveless sea.
For Kilmeny had been she knew not where,
And Kilmeny had seen what she could not declare;
Kilmeny had been where the cock never crew,   40
Where the rain never fell, and the wind never blew,
But it seemed as the harp of the sky had rung,
And the airs of heaven played round her tongue,
When she spake of the lovely forms she had seen,
And a land where sin had never been;   45

A land of love, and a land of light,
Withouten sun, or moon, or night:
Where the river swa'd a living stream,
And the light a pure celestial beam:
The land of vision it would seem,   50
A still, an everlasting dream.

  In yon green-wood there is a waik,
And in that waik there is a wene,
  And in that wene there is a maike,
That neither has flesh, blood, nor bane;   55
  And down in yon green-wood he walks his lane.

  In that green wene Kilmeny lay,
Her bosom happed wi' the flowerits gay;
But the air was soft and the silence deep,
And bonny Kilmeny fell sound asleep.   60
She kend nae mair, nor opened her ee,
Till waked by the hymns of a far countrye.

  She 'wakened on couch of the silk sae slim,
All striped wi' the bars of the rainbow's rim;
And lovely beings round were rife,   65
Who erst had travelled mortal life;
And aye they smiled, and 'gan to speer,
"What spirit has brought this mortal here?"—

  "Lang have I journeyed the world wide,"
A meek and reverend fere replied;   70
"Baith night and day I have watched the fair,
Eident a thousand years and mair.
Yes, I have watched o'er ilk degree,
Wherever blooms femenitye;
But sinless virgin, free of stain   75
In mind and body, fand I nane.

Never, since the banquet of time,
Found I a virgin in her prime,
Till late this bonny maiden I saw
As spotless as the morning snaw: 80
Full twenty years she has lived as free
As the spirits that sojourn this countrye.
I have brought her away frae the snares of men,
That sin or death she never may ken."—

They clasped her waiste and her hands sae fair,   85
They kissed her cheek, and they kemed her hair,
And round came many a blooming fere,
Saying, "Bonny Kilmeny, ye're welcome here!
Women are freed of the littand scorn:
O, blessed be the day Kilmeny was born!   90
Now shall the land of the spirits see,
Now shall it ken what a woman may be!
Many a lang year in sorrow and pain,
Many a lang year through the world we've gane,
Commissioned to watch fair womankind,   95
For its they who nurice th'immortal mind.
We have watched their steps as the dawning shone,
And deep in the green-wood walks alone;
By lilly bower and silken bed,
The viewless tears have o'er them shed;   100
Have soothed their ardent minds to sleep,
Or left the couch of love to weep.
We have seen! we have seen! but the time must come,
And the angels will weep at the day of doom!

"O, would the fairest of mortal kind   105
Aye keep the holy truths in mind,
That kindred spirits their motions see,
Who watch their ways with anxious ee,

And grieve for the guilt of humanitye!
O, sweet to Heaven the maiden's prayer,   110
And the sigh that heaves a bosom sae fair!
And dear to Heaven the words of truth,
And the praise of virtue frae beauty's mouth!
And dear to the viewless forms of air,
The minds that kyth as the body fair!   115

"O, bonny Kilmeny! free frae stain,
If ever you seek the world again,
That world of sin, of sorrow and fear,
O, tell of the joys that are waiting here;
And tell of the signs you shall shortly see;   120
Of the times that are now, and the times that shall
      be."—

They lifted Kilmeny, they led her away,
And she walked in the light of a sunless day:
The sky was a dome of crystal bright,
The fountain of vision, and fountain of light: 125
The emerald fields were of dazzling glow,
And the flowers of everlasting blow.
Then deep in the stream her body they laid,
That her youth and beauty never might fade;
And they smiled on heaven, when they saw her lie 130
In the stream of life that wandered bye.
And she heard a song, she heard it sung,
She kend not where; but sae sweetly it rung,
It fell on her ear like a dream of the morn:
"O! blest be the day Kilmeny was born!   135
Now shall the land of the spirits see,
Now shall it ken what a woman may be!
The sun that shines on the world sae bright,
A borrowed gleid frae the fountain of light;

And the moon that sleeks the sky sae dun,   140
Like a gouden bow, or a beamless sun,
Shall wear away, and be seen nae mair,
And the angels shall miss them travelling the air.
But lang, lang after baith night and day,
When the sun and the world have elyed away;   145
When the sinner has gane to his waesome doom,
Kilmeny shall smile in eternal bloom!"—

They bore her away she wist not how,
For she felt not arm nor rest below;
But so swift they wained her through the light,   150
'Twas like the motion of sound or sight;
They seemed to split the gales of air,
And yet nor gale nor breeze was there.
Unnumbered groves below them grew,
They came, they past, and backward flew,   155
Like floods of blossoms gliding on,
In moment seen, in moment gone.
O, never vales to mortal view
Appeared like those o'er which they flew!
That land to human spirits given,   160
The lowermost vales of the storied heaven;
From thence they can view the world below,
And heaven's blue gates with sapphires glow,
More glory yet unmeet to know.

They bore her far to a mountain green,   165
To see what mortal never had seen;
And they seated her high on a purple sward,
And bade her heed what she saw and heard,
And note the changes the spirits wrought,
For now she lived in the land of thought.   170

She looked, and she saw nor sun nor skies,
But a crystal dome of a thousand dies.
She looked, and she saw nae land aright,
But an endless whirl of glory and light.
And radiant beings went and came   175
Far swifter than wind, or the linked flame.
She hid her een frae the dazzling view;
She looked again and the scene was new.

She saw a sun on a summer sky,
And clouds of amber sailing bye;   180
A lovely land beneath her lay,
And that land had glens and mountains gray;
And that land had vallies and hoary piles,
And marled seas, and a thousand isles;
Its fields were speckled, its forests green,   185
And its lakes were all of the dazzling sheen,
Like magic mirrors, where slumbering lay
The sun and the sky and the cloudlet gray;
Which heaved and trembled and gently swung,
On every shore they seemed to be hung;   190
For there they were seen on their downward plain
A thousand times and a thousand again;
In winding lake and placid firth,
Little peaceful heavens in the bosom of earth.

Kilmeny sighed and seemed to grieve,   195
For she found her heart to that land did cleave;
She saw the corn wave on the vale,
She saw the deer run down the dale;
She saw the plaid and the broad claymore,
And the brows that the badge of freedom bore;   200
And she thought she had seen the land before.

She saw a lady sit on a throne,
The fairest that ever the sun shone on!
A lion licked her hand of milk,
And she held him in a leish of silk;   205
And a leifu' maiden stood at her knee,
With a silver wand and melting ee;
Her sovereign shield till love stole in,
And poisoned all the fount within.

Then a gruff untoward bedeman came,   210
And hundit the lion on his dame:
And the guardian maid wi' the dauntless ee,
She dropped a tear, and left her knee;
And she saw till the queen frae the lion fled,
Till the bonniest flower of the world lay dead.   215
A coffin was set on a distant plain,
And she saw the red blood fall like rain:
Then bonny Kilmeny's heart grew sair,
And she turned away, and could look nae mair.

Then the gruff grim carle girned amain,   220
And they trampled him down, but he rose again;
And he baited the lion to deeds of weir,
Till he lapped the blood to the kingdom dear;
And weening his head was danger-preef,
When crowned with the rose and clover leaf,   225
He gowled at the carle, and chased him away
To feed wi' the deer on the mountain gray.
He gowled at the carle, and he gecked at heaven,
But his mark was set, and his arles given.
Kilmeny a while her een withdrew;   230
She looked again, and the scene was new.

She saw below her fair unfurled
One half of all the glowing world,
Where oceans rolled, and rivers ran,
To bound the aims of sinful man.   235
She saw a people, fierce and fell,
Burst frae their bounds like fiends of hell;
There lilies grew, and the eagle flew,
And she herked on her ravening crew,
Till the cities and towers were wrapt in a blaze,   240
And the thunder it roared o'er the lands and the seas.
The widows they wailed, and the red blood ran,
And she threatened an end to the race of man:
She never lened, nor stood in awe,
Till claught by the lion's deadly paw.   245
Oh! then the eagle swinked for life,
And brainzelled up a mortal strife;
But flew she north, or flew she south,
She met wi' the gowl of the lion's mouth.

With a mooted wing and waefu' maen,   250
The eagle sought her eiry again;
But lang may she cour in her bloody nest,
And lang, lang sleek her wounded breast,
Before she sey another flight,
To play wi' the norland lion's might.   255

But to sing the sights Kilmeny saw,
So far surpassing nature's law,
The singer's voice wad sink away,
And the string of his harp wad cease to play.
But she saw till the sorrows of man were bye,   260
And all was love and harmony;
Till the stars of heaven fell calmly away,
Like the flakes of snaw on a winter day.

Then Kilmeny begged again to see
The friends she had left in her own country,   265
To tell of the place where she had been,
And the glories that lay in the land unseen;
To warn the living maidens fair,
The loved of Heaven, the spirits' care,
That all whose minds unmeled remain   270
Shall bloom in beauty when time is gane.

With distant music, soft and deep,
They lulled Kilmeny sound asleep;
And when she awakened, she lay her lane,
All happed with flowers in the green-wood wene.   275
When seven lang years had come and fled;
When grief was calm, and hope was dead;
When scarce was remembered Kilmeny's name,
Late, late in a gloamin Kilmeny came hame!
And O, her beauty was fair to see,   280
But still and stedfast was her ee!
Such beauty bard may never declare,
For there was no pride nor passion there;
And the soft desire of maidens een
In that mild face could never be seen.   285
Her seymar was the lilly flower,
And her cheek the moss-rose in the shower;
And her voice like the distant melodye,
That floats along the twilight sea.
But she loved to raike the lanely glen,   290
And keeped afar frae the haunts of men;
Her holy hymns unheard to sing,
To suck the flowers, and drink the spring.
But wherever her peaceful form appeared,
The wild beasts of the hill were cheered;   295

The wolf played blythly round the field,
The lordly byson lowed and kneeled;
The dun deer wooed with manner bland,
And cowered aneath her lilly hand.
And when at even the woodlands rung,   300
When hymns of other worlds she sung,
In ecstacy of sweet devotion,
O, then the glen was all in motion.
The wild beasts of the forest came,
Broke from their bughts and faulds the tame,   305
And goved around, charmed and amazed;
Even the dull cattle crooned and gazed,
And murmured and looked with anxious pain
For something the mystery to explain.
The buzzard came with the throstle-cock;   310
The corby left her houf in the rock;
The blackbird alang wi' the eagle flew;
The hind came tripping o'er the dew;
The wolf and the kid their raike began,
And the tod, and the lamb, and the leveret ran;   315
The hawk and the hern attour them hung,
And the merl and the mavis forhooyed their young;
And all in a peaceful ring were hurled:
It was like an eve in a sinless world!

When a month and a day had come and gane,   320
Kilmeny sought the greenwood wene;
There laid her down on the leaves sae green,
And Kilmeny on earth was never mair seen.
But O, the words that fell from her mouth,
Were words of wonder, and words of truth!   325
But all the land were in fear and dread,
For they kendna whether she was living or dead.

It wasna her hame, and she couldna remain;
She left this world of sorrow and pain,
And returned to the land of thought again.   330

FROM THE CONCLUSION

Now, my loved Harp, a while farewell;
    I leave thee on the old gray thorn;
The evening dews will mar thy swell,
    That waked to joy the cheerful morn.

Farewell, sweet soother of my woe!   5
    Chill blows the blast around my head;
And louder yet that blast may blow,
    When down this weary vale I've sped.

The wreath lies on Saint Mary's shore;
    The mountain sounds are harsh and loud;   10
The lofty brows of stern Clokmore
    Are visored with the moving cloud.

But Winter's deadly hues shall fade
    On moorland bald and mountain shaw,
And soon the rainbow's lovely shade   15
    Sleep on the breast of Bowerhope Law;

Then will the glowing suns of spring,
    The genial shower and stealing dew,
Wake every forest bird to sing,
    And every mountain flower renew.   20

But not the rainbow's ample ring,
    That spans the glen and mountain grey,
Though fanned by western breeze's wing,
    And sunned by summer's glowing ray,

To man decayed, can ever more   25
   Renew the age of love and glee!
Can ever second spring restore
   To my old mountain Harp and me!

But when the hue of softened green
   Spreads over hill and lonely lea,   30
And lowly primrose opes unseen
   Her virgin bosom to the bee;

When hawthorns breathe their odours far,
   And carols hail the year's return;
And daisy spreads her silver star   35
   Unheeded by the mountain burn;

Then will I seek the aged thorn,
   The haunted wild and fairy ring,
Where oft thy erring numbers borne
   Have taught the wandering winds to sing.   40

END OF THE QUEEN'S WAKE

NOTES[1]

———

'Introduction'

85–8   *Those wakes, now played by minstrels poor,*
        At midnight's darkest, chillest hour,
        Those humble wakes, now scorned by all,
        Were first begun in courtly hall.

In former days, the term *Wake* was only used to distinguish the festive meeting which took place on the evening previous to the dedication of any particular church or chapel. The company sat up all the night, and, in England, amused themselves in various ways, as their inclinations were by habit or study directed. In Scotland, however, which was always the land of music and of song, music and song were the principal, often the only, amusements of the Wake. These songs were generally of a sacred or serious nature, and were chanted to the old simple melodies of the country. *The Bush aboon Traquair, The Broom of Cowdenknows, John come kiss me now,* and many others, are still extant, set to the Psalms of David, and other spiritual songs, the Psalms being turned into a rude metre corresponding to the various measures of the tunes.

The difference in the application of the term which exists in the two sister kingdoms, sufficiently explains the consequences of the wakes in either. In England they have given rise to many fairs and festivals of long standing; and, from that origin, every fair or festival is denominated a *wake*. In Scotland the term is not used to distinguish any thing either subsistent or relative, save those serenades played by itinerant and nameless minstrels in the streets and squares of Edinburgh, which are inhabited by the great and wealthy, after midnight, about the time of the Christmas holidays. These seem to be the only remainder of the ancient wakes now in Scotland, and their effect upon a mind that delights in music is soothing and delicious beyond all previous conception. A person who can relish the concord

[1] These notes by Hogg were printed at the end of the early editions of *The Queen's Wake.*

of sweet sounds, gradually recalled from sleep by the music of the
wakes, of which he had no previous anticipation, never fails of being
deprived, for a considerable time, of all recollection, what condition,
what place, or what world he is in. The minstrels who, in the reign of
the Stuarts, enjoyed privileges which were even denied to the prin-
cipal nobility, were, by degrees, driven from the tables of the great
to the second, and afterwards to the common hall, that their music
and songs might be heard, while they themselves were unseen. From
the common hall they were obliged to retire to the porch or court;
and so low has the characters of the minstrels descended, that the
performers of the Christmas wakes are wholly unknown to the most
part of those whom they serenade. They seem to be despised, but
enjoy some small privileges, in order to keep up a name of high and
ancient origin.

173–6   *There rode the lords of France and Spain,*
               Of England, Flanders, and Lorraine,
               While serried thousands round them stood,
               From shore of Leith to Holyrood.

Hollingshed describes Queen Mary's landing in Scotland, with her
early misfortunes and accomplishments after this manner: "She
arrived at Leith the 20th of August, in the year of our Lord 1561,
where she was honourably received by the Earl of Argyle, the Lord
Erskine, the Prior of St Andrew's, and the burgesses of Edinburgh,
and conveyed to the Abbie of Holie-rood-house, for (as saith
Buchanan) when some had spread abroad her landing in Scotland,
the nobility and others assembled out of all parts of the realme, as it
were to a common spectacle.

"This did they, partly to congratulate her return, and partly to
shew the dutie which they alwais bear unto her (when she was absent),
either to have thanks therefore, or to prevent the slanders of the
enemies: wherefore not a few, by these beginnings of her reign, did
gesse what would follow, although, in those so variable notions of the
minds of the people, every one was very desirous to see their Queen
offered unto them (unlooked for), after so many haps of both fortunes
as had befallen her. For, when she was but six days old, she lost her
father among the cruel tempests of battle, and was, with great
diligence, brought up by her mother (being a chosen and worthy
person), but yet left as a prize to others, by reason of civil sedition
in Scotland, and of outward wars with other nations, being further

led abroad to all the dangers of frowning fortune, before she could know what evil did mean.

"For leaving her own country, she was nourished as a banished person, and hardly preserved in life from the weapons of her enemies, and violence of the seas. After which fortune began to flatter her, in that she honoured her with a worthy marriage, which, in truth, was rather a shadow of joie to this queen, than any comfort at all. For, shortly after the same, all things were turned to sorrow, by the death of her new young husband, and of her old and grieved mother, by loss of her new kingdom, and by the doubtful possession of her old heritable realme. But as for these things she was both pitied and praised, so was she also for gifts of nature as much beloved and favoured, in that beneficial nature (or rather good God) had indued her with a beautiful face, a well composed body, an excellent wit, a mild nature, and good behaviour, which she had artificially furthered by courtly education, and affable demeanor. Whereby, at the first sight, she wan unto her the hearts of most, and confirmed the love of her faithful subjects."—*Holl.* p. 314. Arbroath Ed. [i.e. *The Scottish Chronicle* . . . by . . . Raphael Hollinshead (2 vols., Arbroath, 1805), vol. 2, pp. 314–15.—*Ed.*]

With regard to the music, which so deeply engaged her attention, we have different accounts by contemporaries, and those at complete variance with one another. Knox says, "Fyres of joy were set furth at night, and a companie of maist honest men, with instruments of musick, gave ther salutation at hir chalmer windo: the melodie, as sche alledged, lyked her weill, and sche willed the sam to be continued sum nychts efter with grit diligence." But Dufresnoy, who was one of the party who accompanied the Queen, gives a very different account of these Scottish minstrels. "We landed at Leith," says he, "and went from thence to Edinburgh, which is but a short league distant. The Queen went there on horse-back, and the lords and ladies who accompanied her upon the little wretched hackneys of the country, as wretchedly capparisoned; at sight of which the Queen began to weep, and to compare them with the pomp and superb palfreys of France. But there was no remedy but patience. What was worst of all, being arrived at Edinburgh, and retired to rest in the Abbey (which is really a fine building, and not at all partaking of the rudeness of that country), there came under her window a crew of five or six hundred scoundrels from the city, who gave her a serenade with wretched violins and little rebecks, of which there are enough in that country, and began to sing Psalms so miserably mistimed and mistuned, that nothing could be worse. Alas! what music! and what a night's rest!"

This Frenchman has had no taste for Scottish music—such another concert is certainly not in record.

[The quotation from Knox is taken from Book IV of *The History of the Reformation in Scotland*. The quotation from 'Dufresnoy' is a translation of part of the life of Mary Queen of Scots in *Les Vies des Dames Illustres* by Pierre de Bourdeille, Seigneur de Brantôme.—*Ed.*]

'The Witch of Fife'

It may suffice to mention, once for all, that the catastrophe of this tale, as well as the principal events related in the tales of *Old David* and *M'Gregor*, are all founded on popular traditions. So is also the romantic story of Kilmeny's disappearance and revisiting her friends, after being seven years in Fairyland. The tradition bears some resemblance to the old ballads of Tam Lean and Thomas of Erceldon; and it is not improbable that all the three may have drawn their origin from the same ancient romance.

'Kilmeny'

Beside the old tradition on which this ballad is founded, there are some modern incidents of a similar nature, which cannot well be accounted for, yet are as well attested as any occurrence that has taken place in the present age. The relation may be amusing to some readers.

A man in the parish of Traquair, and county of Peebles, was busied one day casting turf in a large open field opposite to the mansion-house—the spot is well known, and still pointed out as rather unsafe; his daughter, a child seven years of age, was playing beside him, and amusing him with her prattle. Chancing to ask a question at her, he was surprised at receiving no answer, and, looking behind him, he perceived that his child was not there. He always averred that, as far as he could remember, she had been talking to him about half a minute before; he was certain it was not above a whole one at most. It was in vain that he ran searching all about like one distracted, calling her name;—no trace of her remained. He went home in a state of mind that may be better conceived than expressed, and raised the people of the parish, who searched for her several days with the same success. Every pool in the river, every bush and den on the mountains around was searched in vain. It was remarked that the father never much encouraged the search, being thoroughly persuaded that she was carried away by some invisible being, else she could not have vanished so suddenly. As a last resource, he applied to the minister of Inverlethen, a neighbouring divine of exemplary piety and zeal in religious matters, who enjoined him to cause prayers be offered to God for her in seven Christian churches, next Sabbath, at the same instant of time; "and then," said he, "if she is dead, God will forgive our sin in praying for the dead, as we do it through ignorance; and if she is still alive, I will answer for it, that all the devils in hell shall be unable to keep her." The injunction was punctually attended to. She was remembered in the prayers of all the neighbouring congregations, next Sunday, at the same hour, and never were there such prayers for fervour heard before. There was one divine in particular, Mr Davidson, who prayed in such a manner that all the hearers trembled. As the old divine foreboded, so it fell out. On that very day, and within an hour of the time on which these prayers were offered, the girl was found, in the Plora wood, sitting, picking the bark from a tree. She could give no perfect account of the circumstances which had befallen to her, but she said she did not want plenty of meat, for that her mother came and fed her with milk and bread several times a-day, and sung her to sleep at night. Her skin had acquired a bluish cast, which wore gradually off in the course of a few weeks. Her name was Jane Brown, she lived to a very advanced age, and was known to many still alive. Every circumstance of this story is truth, if the father's report of the suddenness of her disappearance may be relied on.

Another circumstance, though it happened still later, is not less remarkable. A shepherd of Tushilaw, in the parish of Ettrick, whose name was Walter Dalgleish, went out to the heights of that farm, one Sabbath morning, to herd the young sheep for his son, and let him to church. He took his own dinner along with him, and his son's breakfast. When the sermons were over, the lad went straight home, and did not return to his father. Night came, but nothing of the old shepherd appeared. When it grew very late his dog came home— seemed terrified, and refused to take any meat. The family were ill at ease during the night, especially as they never had known his dog leave him before; and early next morning the lad arose and went to the height to look after his father and his flock. He found his sheep all scattered, and his father's dinner unbroken, lying on the same spot where they had parted the day before. At the distance of 20 yards from the spot, the plaid which the old man wore was lying as if it had been flung from him, and a little farther on, in the same direction, his bonnet was found, but nothing of himself. The country people, as on all such occasions, rose in great numbers, and searched for him many days. My father, and several old men still alive, were of the party. He could not be found or heard of, neither dead nor alive, and at length they gave up all thoughts of ever seeing him more.

On the 20th day after his disappearance, a shepherd's wife, at a place called Berry-bush, came in as the family was sitting down to dinner, and said, that if it were possible to believe that Walter Dalgleish was still in existence, she would say yonder was he coming down the hill. They all ran out to watch the phenomenon, and as the person approached nigher, they perceived that it was actually he, walking without his plaid and his bonnet. The place where he was first descried is not a mile distant from that where he was last seen, and there is neither brake, hag, nor bush. When he came into the house, he shook hands with them all—asked for his family, and spoke as if he had been absent for years, and as if convinced something had befallen them. As they perceived something singular in his looks and manner, they unfortunately forebore asking him any questions at first, but desired him to sit and share their dinner. This he readily complied with, and began to sup some broth with seeming eagerness. He had only taken one or two spoonfuls when he suddenly stopped, a kind of rattling noise was heard in his breast, and he sunk back in a faint. They put him to bed, and from that time forth, he never spoke another word that any person could make sense of. He was removed to his own home, where he lingered a few weeks, and then died. What befel him remains to this day a mystery, and for ever must.

[Hogg concludes his notes to *The Queen's Wake* by glossing the following words: *coomb, shaw, law, glen, strone, ben, dale, wale, cory* or *correi*. He goes on as follows.—*Ed.*]

If there is any other word or term peculiar to Scotland, I am not aware of it. The Songs of the two bards, indeed, who affect to imitate the ancient manner, abound with old Scotch words and terms, which, it is presumed, the rhythm, the tenor of the verse, and the narrative, will illustrate, though they may not be found in any glossary of that language. These are, indeed, generally so notoriously deficient and absurd, that it is painful for anyone conversant in the genuine old provincial dialect to look into them.

Ignorant, however, as I am of every dialect save my mother tongue, I imagine that I understand so much of the English language as to perceive that its muscular strength consists in the energy of its primitive stem—in the trunk from which all its foliage hath sprung, and around which its exuberant tendrils are all entwined and interwoven—I mean the remains of the ancient Teutonic. On the strength of this conceived principle, which may haply be erroneous, I have laid it down as a maxim, that the greater number of these old words and terms that can be introduced with propriety into our language, the better. To this my casual innovations must be attributed. The authority of Grahame and Scott has of late rendered a few of these old terms legitimate. If I had been as much master of the standard language as they, I would have introduced ten times more.

FROM THE POETIC MIRROR

FURTHER EXTRACT FROM
"THE RECLUSE," A POEM

THE FLYING TAILOR

I F ever chance or choice thy footsteps lead
Into that green and flowery burial-ground
That compasseth with sweet and mournful smiles
The church of Grassmere,—by the eastern gate
Enter—and underneath a stunted yew,　　　　　5
Some three yards distant from the gravel-walk,
On the left-hand side, thou wilt espy a grave,
With unelaborate head-stone beautified,
Conspicuous 'mid the other stoneless heaps
'Neath which the children of the valley lie.　　10
There pause—and with no common feelings read
This short inscription—"Here lies buried
The Flying Tailor, aged twenty-nine!"

　Him from his birth unto his death I knew,
And many years before he had attain'd　　　　15
The fulness of his fame, I prophesied
The triumphs of that youth's agility,
And crown'd him with that name which afterwards
He nobly justified—and dying left

To fame's eternal blazon—read it here—   20
"The Flying Tailor!"
               It is somewhat strange
That his mother was a cripple, and his father
Long way declined into the vale of years
When their son Hugh was born. At first the babe
Was sickly, and a smile was seen to pass   25
Across the midwife's cheek, when, holding up
The sickly wretch, she to the father said,
"A fine man-child!" What else could they expect?
The mother being, as I said before,
A cripple, and the father of the child   30
Long way declined into the vale of years.

   But mark the wondrous change—ere he was put
By his mother into breeches, Nature strung
The muscular part of his economy
To an unusual strength, and he could leap,   35
All unimpeded by his petticoats,
Over the stool on which his mother sat
When carding wool, or cleansing vegetables,
Or meek performing other household tasks.
Cunning he watch'd his opportunity,   40
And oft, as house-affairs did call her thence,
Overleapt Hugh, a perfect whirligig,
More than six inches o'er th' astonished stool.
What boots it to narrate, how at leap-frog
Over the breech'd and unbreech'd villagers   45
He shone conspicuous? Leap-frog do I say?
Vainly so named. What though in attitude
The Flying Tailor aped the croaking race
When issuing from the weed-entangled pool,
Tadpoles no more, they seek the new-mown fields, 50

A jocund people, bouncing to and fro'
Amid the odorous clover—while amazed
The grasshopper sits idle on the stalk
With folded pinions and forgets to sing.
Frog-like, no doubt, in attitude he was;   55
But sure his bounds across the village green
Seem'd to my soul—(my soul for ever bright
With purest beams of sacred poesy)
Like bounds of red-deer on the Highland-hill,
When, close-environed by the tinchel's chain,   60
He lifts his branchy forehead to the sky,
Then o'er the many-headed multitude
Springs belling half in terror, half in rage,
And fleeter than the sunbeam or the wind
Speeds to his cloud-lair on the mountain-top.   65

No more of this—suffice it to narrate,
In his tenth year he was apprenticed
Unto a Master Tailor by a strong
And regular indenture of seven years,
Commencing from the date the parchment bore,   70
And ending on a certain day, that made
The term complete of seven solar years.
Oft have I heard him say, that at this time
Of life he was most wretched; for, constrain'd
To sit all day cross-legg'd upon a board,   75
The natural circulation of the blood
Thereby was oft impeded, and he felt
So numb'd at times, that when he strove to rise
Up from his work he could not, but fell back
Among the shreds and patches that bestrew'd   80
With various colours, brightening gorgeously,
The board all round him—patch of warlike red

With which he patched the regimental-suits
Of a recruiting military troop,
At that time stationed in a market town 85
At no great distance—eke of solemn black
Shreds of no little magnitude, with which
The parson's Sunday-coat was then repairing,
That in the new-roof'd church he might appear
With fitting dignity—and gravely fill 90
The sacred seat of pulpit eloquence,
Chearing with doctrinal point and words of faith
The poor man's heart, and from the shallow wit
Of atheist drying up each argument,
Or sharpening his own weapons only to turn 95
Their point against himself, and overthrow
His idols with the very enginery
Reared 'gainst the structure of our English church.

Oft too, when striving all he could to finish
The stated daily task, the needle's point, 100
Slanting insidious from th' eluded stitch,
Hath pinch'd his finger, by the thimble's mail
In vain defended, and the crimson blood
Distain'd the lining of some wedding-suit,
A dismal omen! that to mind like his, 105
Apt to perceive in slightest circumstance
Mysterious meaning, yielded sore distress
And feverish peturbation, so that oft
He scarce could eat his dinner—nay, one night
He swore to run from his apprenticeship, 110
And go on board a first-rate man-of-war,
From Plymouth lately come to Liverpool,
Where, in the stir and tumult of a crew
Composed of many nations, 'mid the roar

Of wave and tempest, and the deadlier voice   115
Of battle, he might strive to mitigate
The fever that consumed his mighty heart.

But other doom was his. That very night
A troop of tumblers came into the village,
Tumbler, equestrian, mountebank,—on wire,   120
On rope, on horse, with cup and balls, intent
To please the gaping multitude, and win
The coin from labour's pocket—small perhaps
Each separate piece of money, but when join'd
Making a good round sum, destined ere long   125
All to be melted, (so these lawless folk
Name spending coin in loose debauchery)
Melted into ale—or haply stouter cheer,
Gin diuretic, or the liquid flame
Of baneful brandy, by the smuggler brought   130
From the French coast in shallop many-oar'd,
Skulking by night round headland and through bay,
Afraid of the King's cutter, or the barge
Of cruising frigate, arm'd with chosen men,
And with her sweeps across the foamy waves   135
Moving most beautiful with measured strokes.

It chanced that as he threw a somerset
Over three horses (each of larger size
Than our small mountain-breed) one of the troop
Put out his shoulder, and was otherwise   140
Considerably bruised, especially
About the loins and back. So he became
Useless unto that wandering company,
And likely to be felt a sore expence
To men just on the eve of bankruptcy;   145

So the master of the troop determined
To leave him in the work-house, and proclaim'd
That if there was a man among the crowd
Willing to fill his place and able too,
Now was the time to shew himself. Hugh Thwaites   150
Heard the proposal, as he stood apart
Striving with his own soul—and with a bound
He leapt into the circle, and agreed
To supply the place of him who had been hurt.
A shout of admiration and surprise   155
Then tore heaven's concave, and completely fill'd
The little field, where near a hundred people
Were standing in a circle round and fair.
Oft have I striven by meditative power,
And reason working 'mid the various forms   160
Of various occupations and professions,
To explain the cause of one phenomenon,
That since the birth of science hath remain'd
A bare enunciation, unexplain'd
By any theory, or mental light   165
Stream'd on it by the imaginative will,
Or spirit musing in the cloudy shrine
The Penetralia of the immortal soul.
I now allude to that most curious fact,
That 'mid a given number, say threescore,   170
Of tailors, more men of agility
Will issue out, than from an equal shew
From any other occupation—say
Smiths, barbers, bakers, butchers, or the like.
Let me not seem presumptuous, if I strive   175
This subject to illustrate; nor, while I give
My meditations to the world, will I
Conceal from it, that much I have to say

I learnt from one who knows the subject well
In theory and practice—need I name him?   180
The light-heel'd author of the Isle of Palms,
Illustrious more for leaping than for song.

    First, then, I would lay down this principle,
That all excessive action by the law
Of nature tends unto repose. This granted,   185
All action not excessive must partake
The nature of excessive action—so
That in all human beings who keep moving,
Unconscious cultivation of repose
Is going on in silence. Be it so.   190
Apply to men of sedentary lives
This leading principle, and we behold
That, active in their inactivity,
And unreposing in their long repose,
They are, in fact, the sole depositaries   195
Of all the energies by others wasted,
And come at last to teem with impulses
Of muscular motion, not to be withstood,
And either giving vent unto themselves
In numerous feats of wild agility,   200
Or terminating in despair and death.

    Now of all sedentary lives, none seems
So much so as the tailor's.—Weavers use
Both arms and legs, and, we may safely add,
Their bodies too, for arms and legs can't move   205
Without the body—as the waving branch
Of the green oak disturbs his glossy trunk.
Not so the Tailor—for he sits cross-legg'd,
Cross-legg'd for ever! save at time of meals,

In bed, or when he takes his little walk   210
From shop to alehouse, picking as he goes
Stray patch of fustian, cloth, or cassimere,
Which, as by natural instinct, he discerns,
Though soil'd with mud, and by the passing wheel
Bruised to attenuation 'gainst the stones.   215

   Here then we pause—and need no farther go,
We have reach'd the sea-mark of our utmost sail.
Now let me trace the effect upon his mind
Of this despised profession. Deem not thou,
O rashly deem not, that his boyish days   220
Past at the shop-board, when the stripling bore
With bashful feeling of apprenticeship
The name of Tailor, deem not that his soul
Derived no genial influence from a life,
Which, although haply adverse in the main   225
To the growth of intellect, and the excursive power,
Yet in its ordinary forms possess'd
A constant influence o'er his passing thoughts,
Moulded his appetences and his will,
And wrought out, by the work of sympathy,   230
Between his bodily and mental form,
Rare correspondence, wond'rous unity!
Perfect—complete—and fading not away.
While on his board cross-legg'd he used to sit,
Shaping of various garments, to his mind   235
An image rose of every character
For whom each special article was framed,
Coat, waistcoat, breeches. So at last his soul
Was like a storehouse, fill'd with images,
By musing hours of solitude supplied.   240
Nor did his ready fingers shape the cut

Of villager's uncouth habiliments
With greater readiness, than did his mind
Frame corresponding images of those
Whose corporal measurement the neat-mark'd paper 245
In many a mystic notch for aye retain'd.
Hence, more than any man I ever knew,
Did he possess the power intuitive
Of diving into character. A pair
Of breeches to his philosophic eye   250
Were not what unto other folks they seem,
Mere simple breeches, but in them he saw
The symbol of the soul—mysterious, high
Hieroglyphics! such as Egypt's Priest
Adored upon the holy Pyramid,   255
Vainly imagined tomb of monarchs old,
But raised by wise philosophy, that sought
By darkness to illumine, and to spread
Knowledge by dim concealment—process high
Of man's imaginative, deathless soul.   260
Nor, haply, in th' abasement of the life
Which stern necessity had made his own,
Did he not recognize a genial power
Of soul-ennobling fortitude. He heard
Unmoved the witling's shallow contumely,   265
And thus, in spite of nature, by degrees
He saw a beauty and a majesty
In this despised trade, which warrior's brow
Hath rarely circled—so that when he sat
Beneath his sky-light window, he hath cast   270
A gaze of triumph on the godlike sun,
And felt that orb, in all his annual round,
Beheld no happier nobler character
Than him, Hugh Thwaites, a little tailor-boy.

Thus I, with no unprofitable song,   275
Have, in the silence of th' umbrageous wood,
Chaunted the heroic youthful attributes
Of him the Flying Tailor. Much remains
Of highest argument, to lute or lyre
Fit to be murmur'd with impassion'd voice;   280
And when, by timely supper and by sleep
Refresh'd, I turn me to the welcome task,
With lofty hopes,—Reader, do thou expect
The final termination of my lay.
For, mark my words,—eternally my name   285
Shall last on earth, conspicuous like a star
'Mid that bright galaxy of favour'd spirits,
Who, laugh'd at constantly whene'er they publish'd,
Survived the impotent scorn of base Reviews,
Monthly or Quarterly, or that accursed   290
Journal, the Edinburgh Review, that lives
On tears, and sighs, and groans, and brains, and blood.

END OF THE FLYING TAILOR

STILL FURTHER EXTRACT FROM
"THE RECLUSE," A POEM

JAMES RIGG

ON Tuesday morn, at half-past six o'clock,
I rose and dress'd myself, and having shut

The door o' the bed-room still and leisurely,
I walk'd down stairs. When at the outer-door
I firmly grasp'd the key that ere night-fall   5
Had turn'd the lock into its wonted niche
Within the brazen implement, that shone
With no unseemly splendour,—mellow'd light,
Elicited by touch of careful hand
On the brown lintel; and th' obedient door,   10
As at a potent necromancer's touch,
Into the air receded suddenly,
And gave wide prospect of the sparkling lake,
Just then emerging from the snow-white mist
Like angel's veil slow-folded up to heaven.   15
And lo! a vision bright and beautiful
Sheds a refulgent glory o'er the sand,
The sand and gravel of my avenue!
For, standing silent by the kitchen-door,
Tinged by the morning sun, and in its own   20
Brown natural hide most lovely, two long ears
Upstretching perpendicularly, then
With the horizon levell'd—to my gaze
Superb as horn of fabled Unicorn,
Each in its own proportions grander far   25
Than the frontal glory of that wandering beast,
Child of the Desart! Lo! a beauteous Ass,
With panniers hanging silent at each side!
Silent as cage of bird whose song is mute,
Though silent yet not empty, fill'd with bread   30
The staff of life, the means by which the soul
By fate obedient to the powers of sense,
Renews its faded vigour, and keeps up

A proud communion with the eternal heavens.
Fasten'd to a ring it stood, while at its head   35
A boy of six years old, as angel bright,
Patted its neck, and to its mouth applied
The harmless thistle that his hand had pluck'd
From the wild common, melancholy crop.

Not undelightful was that simple sight,   40
For I at once did recognize that ass
To be the property of one James Rigg,
Who for the last seven years had managed,
By a firm course of daily industry,
A numerous family to support, and clothe   45
In plain apparel of our shepherd's grey.
On him a heavy and calamitous lot
Had fallen. For working up among the hills
In a slate-quarry, while he fill'd the stone,
Bored by his cunning with nitrous grain,   50
It suddenly exploded, and the flash
Quench'd the bright lustre of his cheerful eyes
For ever, so that now they roll in vain
To find the searching light that idly plays
O'er the white orbs, and on the silent cheeks   55
By those orbs unilluminated calm and still.

Quoth I, I never see thee and thy ass,
My worthy friend, but I methinks behold
The might of that unconquerable spirit,
Which, operating in the ancient world   60
Before the Flood, when fallen man was driven
From paradise, accompanied him to fields
Bare and unlovely, when the sterile earth
Oft mock'd the kindly culture of the hand
Of scientific agriculture—mock'd   65

The shepherd's sacrifice, and even denied
A scanty pittance to the fisherman,
Who by the rod or net sought to supply
His natural wants from river or from mere.
Blind were these people to the cunning arts   70
Of smooth civility—men before the Flood,
And therefore in the scriptures rightly call'd
Antediluvians!
            While thus I spake
With wisdom, that industrious blind old man,
Seemingly flatter'd by those words of mine,   75
Which, judging by myself, I scarcely think
He altogether understood, replied,
While the last thistle slowly disappear'd
Within the jaws of that most patient beast:
"Master!" quoth he,—and while he spake his hat   80
With something of a natural dignity
Was holden in his hand—"Master," quoth he,
" I hear that you and Mrs Wordsworth think
Of going into Scotland, and I wish
To know if, while the family are from home,   85
I shall supply the servants with their bread,
For I suppose they will not all be put
Upon board-wages."
                Something in his voice,
While thus he spake of simplest articles
Of household use, yet sunk upon my soul,   90
Like distant thunder from the mountain-gloom
Wakening the sleeping echoes, so sublime
Was that old man, so plainly eloquent
His untaught tongue! though something of a lisp,
(Natural defect,) and a slight stutter too   95
(Haply occasion'd by some faint attack,

Harmless, if not renew'd, of apoplex)
Render'd his utterance most peculiar,
So that a stranger, had he heard that voice
Once only, and then travell'd into lands   100
Beyond the ocean, had on his return,
Met where they might, have known that curious voice
Of lisp and stutter, yet I ween withal
Graceful, and breathed from an original mind.

Here let me be permitted to relate,   105
For sake of those few readers who prefer
A simple picture of the heart to all
Poetic imagery from earth or heaven
Drawn by the skill of bard,—let me, I say,
For sake of such few readers, be permitted   110
To tell, in plain and ordinary verse,
What James Rigg first experienced in his soul,
Standing amid the silence of the hills,
With both the pupils of his eyes destroyed.

When first the loud explosion through the sky   115
Sent its far voice, and from the trembling rocks
That with an everlasting canopy
O'ershadow Stickle-Tarn the echoes woke,
So that the mountain-solitude was filled
With sound, as with the air! He stood awhile,   120
Wondering from whence that tumult might proceed,
And all unconscious that the blast had dimm'd
His eyes for ever, and their smiling blue
Converted to a pale and mournful grey.
Was it, he thought, some blast the quarrymen   125
Blasted at Conniston, or in that vale,
Called from its huge and venerable yew,
Yewdale? (though other etymologists

Derive that appellation from the sheep,
Of which the female in our English tongue   130
Still bears the name of ewe.) Or did the gun
Of fowler, wandering o'er the heathery wilds
In search of the shy gor-cock, yield that voice
Close to his ear, so close that through his soul
It rolled like thunder? Or had news arrived   135
Of Buonaparte's last discomfiture,
By the bold Russ, and that great heir of fame
Blucher, restorer of the thrones of kings?
And upon Lowood bowling-green did Laker
Glad of expedient to beguile the hours,   140
Slow moving before dinner, did he fire
In honour of that glorious victory,
The old two-pounder by the wind and rain
Rusted, and seemingly to him more old
Than in reality it was, though old,   145
And on that same green lying since the days
Of the last landlord, Gilbert Ormathwaite,
Name well-remember'd all the country round,
Though twenty summer suns have shed their flowers
On the green turf that hides his mortal dust.   150
Or was it, thought he, the loud signal-gun
Of pleasure-boat, on bright Winander's wave,
Preparing 'gainst some new antagonist
To spread her snowy wings before the wind,
Emulous of glory and the palmy wreath   155
Of inland navigation? graceful sport!
It next perhaps occurr'd to him to ask,
Himself, or some one near him, if the sound
Was not much louder than those other sounds,
Fondly imagined by him,—and both he,   160
And that one near him, instantly replied

Unto himself, that most assuredly
The noise proceeded from the very stone,
Which they two had so long been occupied
In boring, and that probably some spark,   165
Struck from the gavelock 'gainst the treacherous flint,
Had fallen amid the powder, and so caused
The stone t' explode, as gunpowder will do,
With most miraculous force, especially
When close ramm'd down into a narrow bore,   170
And cover'd o'er with a thin layer of sand
To exclude the air, else otherwise the grain,
Escaping from the bore, would waste itself
In the clear sky, and leave the bored stone
Lying unmoved upon the verdant earth,   175
Like some huge creature stretch'd in lazy sleep
Amid the wilderness,—or lying dead
Beneath the silence of the summer sun.

   This point establish'd, he was gently led
By the natural progress of the human soul,   180
Aspiring after truth, nor satisfied
Till she hath found it, wheresoever hid,
(Yea even though at the bottom of a well,)
To enquire if any mischief had been done
By that explosion; and while thus he stood   185
Enquiring anxiously for all around,
A small sharp boy, whose task it was to bring
His father's breakfast to him 'mid the hills,
Somewhat about eleven years of age,
Though less than some lads at the age of eight,   190
Exclaim'd—"Why, father, do you turn the white
Of your eyes up so?" At these simple words
Astonishment and horror struck the souls

Of all the quarrymen, for they descried,
Clear as the noon-day, that James Rigg had lost   195
His eyesight, yea his very eyes were lost,
Quench'd in their sockets, melted into air,
A moisture mournful as the cold dim gleam
Of water sleeping in some shady wood,
Screen'd from the sunbeams and the breath of heaven.   200

On that he lifted up his harden'd hands,
Harden'd by sun, and rain, and storm, and toil,
Unto the blasted eye-balls, and awhile
Stood motionless as fragment of that rock
That wrought him all his woe, and seem'd to lie,   205
Unwitting of the evil it had done,
Calm and serene, even like a flock of sheep,
Scatter'd in sunshine o'er the Cheviot-hills.
I ween that, as he stood in solemn trance,
Tears flow'd for him who wept not for himself,   210
And that his fellow-quarrymen, though rude
Of soul and manner, not untouchingly
Deplored his cruel doom, and gently led
His footsteps to a green and mossy rock,
By sportive Nature fashion'd like a chair,   215
With seat, back, elbows,—a most perfect chair
Of unhewn living rock! There, hapless man,
He moved his lips, as if he inly pray'd,
And clasp'd his hands and raised his sightless face
Unto the smiling sun, who walk'd through heaven,   220
Regardless of that fatal accident,
By which a man was suddenly reduced
From an unusual clear long-sightedness
To utter blindness—blindness without hope,
So wholly were the visual nerves destroyed.   225

"I wish I were at home!" he slowly said,
"For though I ne'er must see that home again,
"I yet may hear it, and a thousand sounds
"Are there to gladden a poor blind man's heart."

He utter'd truth,—lofty, consoling truth!   230
Thanks unto gracious Nature, who hath framed
So wondrously the structure of the soul,
That though it live on outward ministry,
Of gross material objects, by them fed
And nourish'd, even as if th' external world   235
Were the great wet-nurse of the human race,
Yet of such food deprived, she doth not pine
And fret away her mystic energies
In fainting inanition; but, superior
To the food she fed on, in her charge retains   240
Each power, and sense, and faculty, and lives,
Cameleon-like, upon the air serene
Of her own bright imaginative will,
Desiderating nothing that upholds,
Upholds and magnifies, but without eyes   245
Sees—and without the vestige of an ear
Listens, and listening, hears—and without sense
Of touch (if haply from the body's surface
Have gone the sense of feeling) keenly feels,
And in despite of nose abbreviate   250
Smells like a wolf—wolf who for leagues can snuff
The scent of carrion, bird by fowler kill'd,
Kill'd but not found, or little vernal kid
Yean'd in the frost, and soon outstretch'd in death,
White as the snow that serves it for a shroud.   255

Therefore James Rigg was happy, and his face
Soon brighten'd up with smiles, and in his voice

Contentment spoke most musical; so when
The doctor order'd his most worthy wife
To loose the bandage from her husband's eyes,   260
He was so reconciled unto his lot,
That there almost appear'd to him a charm
In blindness—so that, had his sight return'd,
I have good reason to believe his happiness
Had been thereby scarcely at all increased.   265

    While thus confabulating with James Rigg,
Even at that moment when such silence lay
O'er all my cottage, as by mystic power
Belonging to the kingdom of the ear,
O'erthrew at once all old remembrances—   270
Even at that moment, over earth, and air,
The waving forest, and the sleeping lake,
And the far sea of mountains that uplifted
Its stately billows through the clear blue sky,
Came such a sound, as if from her dumb trance   275
Awaken'd Nature, starting suddenly,
Were jealous of insulted majesty,
And sent through continent and trembling isle
Her everlasting thunders. Such a crash
Tore the foundations of the earth, and shook   280
The clouds that slumber'd on the breast of heaven!
It was the parlour-bell that suddenly
An unknown hand had rung. I cast my eyes
Up the long length of bell-rope, and I saw
The visible motion of its iron tongue,   285
By heaven I *saw* it tinkling. Fast at first,
O most unearthly fast, then somewhat slower,
Next very slow indeed, until some four
Or half-a-dozen minutes at the most,

By Time's hand cut from off the shorten'd hour,   290
It stopp'd quite of itself—and idly down,
Like the sear leaf upon th' autumnal bough
Dangled!   *   *   *   *
          *   *   *   *   *

END OF JAMES RIGG

MISCELLANEOUS POEMS

SUPERSTITION

1

In Caledonia's glens there once did reign
 A Sovereign of supreme unearthly eye;
No human power her potence could restrain,
 No human soul her influence deny:
 Sole Empress o'er the mountain homes, that lie 5
Far from the busy world's unceasing stir:
 But gone is her mysterious dignity,
And true Devotion wanes away with her;
While in loose garb appears Corruption's harbinger.

2

Thou sceptic leveller—ill-framed with thee 10
 Is visionary bard a war to wage:
Joy in thy light thou earth-born Saducee,
 That earth is all thy hope and heritage:
 Already wears thy front the line of age;
Thou see'st a heaven above—a grave before; 15
 Does that lone cell thy wishes all engage?
Say, does thy yearning soul not grasp at more?
Woe to thy grovelling creed—thy cold ungenial lore!

3

Be mine to sing of visions that have been,
 And cherish hope of visions yet to be; 20
Of mountains clothed in everlasting green,
 Of silver torrent and of shadowy tree,

Far in the ocean of eternity.
Be mine the faith that spurns the bourn of time;
   The soul whose eye can future glories see;   25
The converse here with things of purer clime,
And hope above the stars that soars on wing sublime.

4

But she is gone that thrilled the simple minds
   Of those I loved and honoured to the last;
She who gave voices to the wandering winds,   30
   And mounted spirits on the midnight blast:
   At her behest the trooping fairies past,
And wayward elves in many a glimmering band;
   The mountains teemed with life, and sore aghast
Stood maid and matron 'neath her mystic wand,   35
When all the spirits rose and walked at her command

5

And she could make the brown and careless boy
   All breathless stand, unknowing what to fear;
Or panting deep beneath his co'erlet lie,
   When midnight whisper stole upon his ear.   40
   And she could mould the vision of the seer
To aught that rankled breast of froward wight;
   Or hang the form of cerement or of bier
Within the cottage fire—O woful sight!
That called forth many a prayer and deepened groan by
     night.   45

6

O! I have bowed to her resistless sway,
   When the thin evening vapours floated nigh;
When the grey plover's wailings died away,
   And the tall mountains melted into sky;

The note of gloaming bee that journeyed bye   50
Sent thro' my heart a momentary knell;
  And sore I feared in bush or brake might lie
Things of unearthly make—for I knew well
That hour with danger fraught more than when mid-
    night fell.

7

But O! if ancient cemetry was near,   55
  Or cairn or harper murdered long ago,
Or wandering pedlar for his hoarded gear,
    Of such, what glen of Scotland doth not know?
    Or grave of suicide (upon the brow
Of the bleak mountain) withered all and grey;   60
    From these I held as from some deadly foe:
There have I quaked by night and mused by day;
But chiefly where I weened the bard or warrior lay.

8

For many a wild heart-thrilling Scottish bard,
  In lowland dale the lyre of heaven that wooed,   65
Sleeps 'neath some little mound or lonely sward,
    Where humble dome of rapt devotion stood;
    'Mid heathy wastes by Mary's silent flood,
Or in the moorland glen of dark Buccleuch;
    There o'er their graves the heath-fowl's mottled brood,   70
Track with light feathery foot the morning dew;
There plays the gamesome lamb, or bleats the yeaning
    ewe.

9

Yet, there still meet the thoughtful shepherd's view
  The marble fount-stone, and the rood so grey;
And often there he sees with changeful hue   75
  The snow-white scull washed by the burn away:

And O! if 'tis his chance at eve to stray,
Lone by the place where his forefathers sleep;
  At bittern's whoop or gor-cock's startling bay,
How heaves his simple breast with breathings deep;   80
He mutters vow to heaven, and speeds along the steep.

10

For well he knows, along that desert room,
  The spirits nightly watch the sacred clay;
That, cradled on the mountain's purple bloom,
  By him they lie companions of the day,   85
  His guardian friends, and listening to his lay:
And many a chaunt floats on the vacant air,
  That spirit of the bard or warrior may
Hear the forgotten names perchance they bare:
For many a warrior wight, and nameless bard lies
    there!   90

11

Those were the times for holiness of frame;
  Those were the days when fancy wandered free;
That kindled in the soul the mystic flame,
  And the rapt breathings of high poesy;
  Sole empress of the twilight—Woe is me!   95
That thou and all thy spectres are outworn;
  For true devotion wanes away with thee.
All thy delirious dreams are laughed to scorn,
While o'er our hills has dawned a cold saturnine morn.

12

Long did thy fairies linger in the wild,   100
  When vale and city wholly were resigned;
Where hoary cliffs o'er little holms were piled,
  And torrents sung their music to the wind:

The darksome heaven upon the hills reclined,
Save when a transient sun-beam, thro' the rain,   105
  Past like some beauteous phantom of the mind
Leaving the hind in solitude again—
These were their last retreats, and heard their parting
    strain.

13

But every vice effeminate has sped,
  Fast as the spirits from our hills have gone,   110
And all these light unbodied forms are fled,
  Or good or evil, save the ghost alone.
  True, when the kine are lowing in the lone,
An evil eye may heinous mischief brew;
  But deep enchantments to the wise are known,   115
That certainly the blasted herd renew,
nd Amake the eldron crone her cantrips sorely rue.

14

O! I have seen the door most closely barred;
  The green turf fire where stuck was many a pin;
The rhymes of incantation I have heard,   120
  And seen the black dish solemnly laid in
  Amid the boiling liquid—Was it sin?
Ah! no—'twas all in fair defence of right.
  With big drops hanging at her brow and chin,
Soon comes the witch in sad and woeful plight;   125
Is cut above the breath, and yelling takes her flight!!

15

And I have seen, in gaunt and famished guise,
  The brindled mouser of the cot appear;
A haggard wildness darted from her eyes:
  No marvel was it when the truth you hear!   130

That she is forced to carry neighbour near,
Swift thro' the night to countries far away;
   That still her feet the marks of travel bear;
And her broad back that erst was sleek and grey,
O! hapless beast!—all galled where the curst saddle lay!   135

16

If every creed has its attendant ills,
   How slight were thine!—a train of airy dreams!
No holy awe the cynic's bosom thrills;
   Be mine the faith diverging to extremes!
   What, though upon the moon's distempered beams,   140
Erewhile thy matrons galloped thro' the heaven,
   Floated like feather on the foaming streams,
Or raised the winds by tenfold fury driven,
Till ocean blurred the sky, and hills in twain were riven.

17

Where fell the scathe?—The beldames were amused,   145
   Whom eld and poverty had sorely crazed;
What, though their feeble senses were abused
   By gleesome demon in the church-aisle raised,
   With lion tail and eyes that baleful blazed!
Whose bagpipe's blare made all the roof to quake!   150
   But ages yet unborn will stand amazed
At thy dread power, that could the wretches make
Believe these things all real, and swear them at the
     stake.

18

But ah! thou filled'st the guilty heart with dread,
   And brought the deeds of darkness to the day!   155
Who was it made the livid corse to bleed
   At murderer's touch, and cause the gelid clay

By fancied movement all the truth betray?
Even from dry bones the drops of blood have sprung!
   'Twas thou Inquisitor!—whose mystic sway   160
A shade of terror over nature hung;
A feeling more sublime than poet ever sung.

19

Fearless the shepherd faced the midnight storm
   To save his flocks deep swathed amid the snow;
Though threatening clouds the face of heaven deform,   165
   The sailor feared not o'er the firth to row;
   Dauntless the hind marched forth to meet the foe:
For why, they knew, though earth and hell combined,
   In heaven were registered their days below;
That there was one well able and inclined   170
To save them from the sword, the wave, and stormy
     wind.

20

O! blissful thought to poverty and age,
   When troubles press and dangers sore belay!
This is their only stay, their anchorage;
   "It is the will of heaven, let us obey!   175
   "Ill it befits the creatures of a day,
"Beneath a father's chastening to repine."
   This high belief in Providence's sway,
In the eye of reason wears into decline;
And soon that heavenly ray must ever cease to shine.   180

21

Yet these were days of marvel—when our king,
   As chronicles and sapient sages tell,
Stood with his priests and nobles in a ring,
   Searching old beldame for the mark of hell.

The test of witchcraft and of devilish spell; 185
And when I see a hag, the country's bane,
   With rancorous heart and tongue of malice fell,
Blight youth and beauty with a burning stain,
I wish for these old times and Stuarts back again.

22

Haply 'tis weened that Scotland now is free 190
   Of witchcraft, and of spell o'er human life.
Ah me!—ne'er since she rose out of the sea,
   Were they so deep, so dangerous, and so rife;
   The heart of man unequal to the strife
Sinks down before the lightning of their eyes. 195
   O! it is meet that every maid and wife
Some keen exorcist still should scrutinize,
And bring them to the test, for all their sorceries.

23

Much have I owed thee—Much may I repine,
   Great Queen! to see thy honours thus decay. 200
Among the mountain maids the power was thine,
   On blest Saint Valantine's or Hallow Day.
   Our's was the omen—their's was to obey:
Firm their belief, or most demurely feigned!
   Each maid her cheek on lover's breast would lay, 205
And, sighing, grant the kiss so long refrained;
'Twas sin to counteract what Providence ordained!

24

O! I remember, as young fancy grew,
   How oft thou spoke'st in voice of distant rill;
What sheeted forms thy plastic finger drew, 210
   Throned on the shadow of the moonlight hill;

Or in the glade so motionless and still
That scarcely in this world I seemed to be;
  High on the tempest sing thine anthem shrill;
Across the heaven upon the meteor flee,   215
Or in the thunder speak with voice of majesty!

25

All these are gone—The days of vision o'er;
  The bard of fancy strikes a tuneless string.
O! if I wist to meet thee here no more,
  My muse should wander on unwearied wing,   220
  To find thy dwelling by some lonely spring,
Where Norway opes her forests to the gale;
  The dell thy home, the cloud thy covering,
The tuneful sea maid, and the spectre pale,
Tending thy gloomy throne, amid heaven's awful veil. 225

26

Or shall I seek thee where the Tana rolls
  Her deep blue torrent to the northern main;
Where many a shade of former huntsman prowls,
  Where summer roses deck th' untrodden plain,
  And beauteous fays and elves, a flickering train,   230
Dance with the foamy spirits of the sea.
  O! let me quake before thee once again,
And take one farewel on my bended knee,
Great ruler of the soul, which none can rule like thee!

FINIS

VERSES ADDRESSED TO
THE RIGHT HONOURABLE
LADY ANNE SCOTT OF BUCCLEUCH

To her, whose bounty oft hath shed
Joy round the peasant's lowly bed,
When trouble press'd and friends were few,
And God and angels only knew:
To her, who loves the board to cheer,   5
And hearth of simple cottager;
Who loves the tale of rural hind,
And wayward visions of his mind,—
I dedicate, with high delight,
The themes of many a winter night.   10

What other name on Yarrow vale
Can Shepherd choose to grace his tale?
There other living name is none
Heard with one feeling—one alone.
Some heavenly charm must name endear   15
That all men love, and all revere!
Even the rude boy of rustic form,
And robe all fluttering to the storm,
Whose roguish lip and graceless eye
Incline to mock the passer by,   20
Walks by the maid with softer tread,
And lowly bends his burly head,
Following with eye of milder ray
The gentle form that glides away.
The little school-nymph, drawing near,   25
Says, with a sly and courteous leer,
As plain as eye and manner can,
"Thou lov'st me—bless thee, Lady Anne!"

Even babes will catch the 'loved theme,
And learn to lisp their Lady's name.   30

   The orphan's blessing rests on thee;
Happy thou art, and long shalt be!
'Tis not in sorrow, nor distress,
Nor fortune's power to make thee less.
The heart, unalter'd in its mood,   35
That joys alone in doing good,
And follows in the heavenly road,
And steps where once an angel trod;—
The joys within such heart that burn,
No loss can quench, nor time o'erturn!   40
The stars may from their orbits bend,
The mountains rock, the heavens rend,
The sun's last ember cool and quiver,
But these shall glow, and glow for ever!

   Then thou, who lov'st the Shepherd's home, 45
And cherishest his lowly dome,
O list the mystic lore sublime
Of fairy tales of ancient time.
I learn'd them in the lonely glen,
The last abodes of living men;   50
Where never stranger came our way
By summer night, or winter day;
Where neighbouring hind or cot was none,
Our converse was with heaven alone,
With voices through the cloud that sung,   55
And brooding storms that round us hung.

   O Lady, judge, if judge you may,
How stern and ample was the sway
Of themes like these, when darkness fell,
And gray-hair'd sires the tales would tell!   60

When doors were barr'd, and eldron dame
Plied at her task beside the flame,
That through the smoke and gloom alone
On dim and umber'd faces shone;
The bleat of mountain goat on high, 65
That from the cliff came quavering by;
The echoing rock, the rushing flood,
The cataract's swell, the moaning wood;
That undefined and mingled hum—
Voice of the desert, never dumb; 70
All these have left within this heart
A feeling tongue can ne'er impart;
A wilder'd and unearthly flame,
A something that's without a name.

And, lady, thou wilt never deem 75
Religious tale offensive theme;
Our creeds may differ in degree,
But small that difference sure can be.
As flowers which vary in their dyes,
We all shall bloom in Paradise. 80
As sire, who loves his children well,
The loveliest face he cannot tell,—
So 'tis with us; we are the same,
One faith, one Father, and one aim.

And hadst thou lived where I was bred, 85
Amid the scenes where martyrs bled,
Their sufferings all to thee endear'd,
By those most honour'd and revered;
And where the wild dark streamlet raves,
Hadst wept above their lonely graves, 90
Thou wouldst have felt, I know it true,
As I have done, and aye must do:

And for the same exalted cause,
For mankind's right, and nature's laws,
The cause of liberty divine,   95
Thy fathers bled as well as mine.

Then be it thine, O noble maid,
On some still eve these tales to read;
And thou wilt read, I know full well,
For still thou lov'st the haunted dell;   100
To linger by the sainted spring,
And trace the ancient fairy ring,
Where moonlight revels long were held
In many a lone sequester'd field,
By Yarrow dens and Ettrick shaw,   105
And the green mounds of Carterhaugh.
O! for one kindred heart, that thought
As minstrel must and lady ought;
That loves, like thee, the whispering wood,
And range of mountain solitude!   110
Think how more wild the mountain scene,
If times were still as they have been;
If fairies, at the fall of even,
Down from the eyebrow of the heaven,
Or some aërial land afar,   115
Came on the beam of rising star;
Their lightsome gambols to renew,
From the green leaf to quaff the dew,
Or dance with such a graceful tread,
As scarce to bend the gowan's head.   120

Think if thou wert, some evening still,
Within thy wood of green Bowhill—
Thy native wood!—the forest's pride!
Lover or sister by thy side;

In converse sweet the hour t' improve,   125
Of things below and things above;
Of an existence scarce begun;
And note the stars rise one by one.
Just then, the moon and day-light blending,
To see the fairy bands descending,   130
Wheeling and shivering as they came,
Like glimmering shreds of human frame;
Or sailing, mid the golden air,
In skiffs of yielding gossamer.
O! I would wander forth alone,   135
Where human eye hath never shone,
Away, o'er continents and isles,
A thousand and a thousand miles,
For one such eve to sit with thee,
Their strains to hear and forms to see!   140
Absent the while all fears of harm,
Secure in Heaven's protecting arm;
To list the songs such beings sung,
And hear them speak in human tongue;
To see in beauty, perfect, pure,   145
Of human face the miniature,
And smile of beings free from sin,
That had not death impress'd within.
Ah! can it ever be forgot,
What Scotland had, and now has not!   150

    Such scenes, dear lady, now no more
Are given, or fitted, as before,
To eye or ear of guilty dust;
But when it comes, as come it must,
The time when I, from earth set free,   155
Shall turn the sprite I fain would be;

If there's a land, as grandsires tell,
Where brownies, elves, and fairies dwell,
There my first visit shall be sped.—
Journeyer of earth, go hide thy head!   160
Of all thy travelling splendour shorn,
Though in thy golden chariot borne!
Yon little cloud of many a hue
That wanders o'er the solar blue,
That curls, and rolls, and fleets away   165
Beyond the very springs of day,
That do I challenge and engage
To be my travelling equipage;
Then onward, onward, far to steer,
The breeze of heaven my charioteer;   170
By azure blue and orient sheen,
By star that glimmers red and green,
And hangs like emerald polish'd bright
Upon the left cheek of the night.
The soul's own energy my guide,   175
Eternal hope my all beside.
At such a shrine who would not bow?
Traveller of earth, where art thou now?

    Then let me for these legends claim
My young, my honour'd Lady's name;   180
That honour is reward complete,
Yet I must crave, if not unmeet,
One little boon—delightful task
For maid to grant, or minstrel ask!

    One day, thou may'st remember well,   185
For short the time since it befel,
When o'er thy forest bowers of oak
The eddying storm in darkness broke;

Loud sung the blast a-down the dell,
And Yarrow lent her treble swell;   190
The mountain's form grew more sublime,
Wrapt in its wreaths of rolling rime;
And Newark cairn, in hoary shroud,
Appear'd like giant o'er the cloud;
The eve fell dark, and grimly scowl'd,   195
Loud and more loud the tempest howl'd;
Without was turmoil, waste, and din,
The kelpie's cry was in the linn!
But all was love and peace within.
And aye between, the melting strain   200
Pour'd from thy woodland harp amain,
Which, mixing with the storm around,
Gave a wild cadence to the sound.

That mingled scene, in every part,
Hath so impress'd thy Shepherd's heart   205
With glowing feelings, kindling, bright,
Some filial visions of delight,
That almost border upon pain,
And he would hear those strains again.
They brought delusions not to last,   210
Blending the future with the past;
Dreams of fair stems, in foliage new,
Of flowers that spring where others grew,
Of beauty ne'er to be outdone,
And stars that rise when sets the sun;   215
The patriarchal days of yore,
The mountain music heard no more,
With all these scenes before his eyes,
A family's and a nation's ties—
Bonds which the heavens alone can rend,   220

With chief, with father, and with friend.
No wonder that such scene refined
Should dwell on rude enthusiast's mind;
Strange his reverse!—he little wist—
Poor inmate of the cloud and mist!   225
That ever he, as friend, should claim
The proudest Caledonian name.

THE MERMAID

"O WHERE won ye, my bonnie lass,
  Wi' look sae wild an' cheery?
There's something in that witching face
  That I lo'e wonder dearly."

"I live where the hare-bell never grew,   5
  Where the streamlet never ran,
Where the winds o' heaven never blew;
  Now find me gin you can."

"'Tis but your wild an' wily way,
  The gloaming maks you eirie,   10
For ye are the lass o' the Braken-Brae,
  An' nae lad maun come near ye:

"But I am sick, an' very sick
  Wi' a passion strange an' new,
For ae kiss o' thy rosy cheek   15
  An' lips o' the coral hue."

"O laith, laith wad a wanderer be
  To do your youth sic wrang,
Were you to reave a kiss from me
  Your life would not be lang.   20

"Go, hie you from this lonely brake,
  Nor dare your walk renew;
For I'm the Maid of the Mountain Lake,
  An' I come wi' the falling dew."

"Be you the Maid of the Crystal Wave,   25
  Or she of the Braken-Brae,
One tender kiss I mean to have;
  You shall not say me nay.

"For beauty's like the daisy's vest
  That shrinks from the early dew,   30
But soon it opes its bonnie breast,
  An' sae may it fare wi' you."

"Kiss but this hand, I humbly sue,
  Even there I'll rue the stain;
O the breath of man will dim its hue,   35
  It will ne'er be pure again.

"For passion's like the burning beal
  Upon the mountain's brow,
That wastes itself to ashes pale;
  An' sae will it fare with you."   40

———————

"O mother, mother, make my bed,
  An' make it soft and easy;
An' with the cold dew bathe my head,
  For pains of anguish seize me:

"Or stretch me in the chill blue lake,   45
  To quench this bosom's burning;
An' lay me by yon lonely brake,
  For hope there's none returning.

"I've been where man should not have been
  Oft in my lonely roaming,   50
And seen what man should not have seen
  By greenwood in the gloaming.

"O, passion's deadlier than the grave,
  A human thing's undoing!
The Maiden of the Mountain Wave   55
  Has lured me to my ruin!"

'Tis now an hundred years an' more,
  An' all these scenes are over,
Since rose his grave on yonder shore,
  Beneath the wild wood cover;   60

An' late I saw the Maiden there,
  Just as the day-light faded,
Braiding her locks of gowden hair,
  An' singing as she braided:—

Mermaid's Song

Lie still, my love, lie still and sleep,   65
  Long is thy night of sorrow;
Thy Maiden of the Mountain Deep
  Shall meet thee on the morrow.

But oh, when shall that morrow be,
  That my true love shall waken?   70
When shall we meet, refined an' free,
  Amid the moorland braken?

Full low and lonely is thy bed,
  The worm even flies thy pillow;
Where now the lips, so comely red,   75
  That kissed me 'neath the willow?

O I must laugh, do as I can,
  Even 'mid my song of mourning,
At all the fuming freaks of man
  To which there's no returning.   80

Lie still, my love, lie still an' sleep—
  Hope lingers o'er thy slumber;
What though thy years beneath the steep
  Should all its stones outnumber?

Though moons steal o'er, an' seasons fly   85
  On time's swift wing unstaying,
Yet there's a spirit in the sky
  That lives o'er thy decaying!

In domes beneath the water-springs
  No end hath my sojourning;   90
An' to this land of fading things
  Far hence be my returning;

For spirits now have left the deep,
  Their long last farewell taking:
Lie still, my love, lie still an' sleep,   95
  Thy day is near the breaking!

When my loved flood from fading day
  No more its gleam shall borrow,
Nor heath-fowl from the moorland grey
  Bid the blue dawn good-morrow;   100

The Mermaid o'er thy grave shall weep,
  Without one breath of scorning:
Lie still, my love, lie still an' sleep!
  And fare thee well till morning!

LINES TO
SIR WALTER SCOTT, BART.

SOUND, my old Harp, thy boldest key
To strain of high festivity!
Can'st thou be silent in the brake,
Loitering by Altrive's mountain lake,
When he who gave the hand its sway   5
That now has tuned thee many a day,
Has gained the honours, trulier won
Than e'er by sword of Albyn's son?
High guerdon of a soul refined,
The meed of an exalted mind!   10

Well suits such wreath thy loyal head,
My counsellor, and friend in deed.
Though hard through life I've pressed my way
For many a chill and joyless day,
Since I have lived enrapt to hail   15
My sovereign's worth, my friend's avail,
And see what more I prize than gain,
Our Forest harp the bays obtain,
I'll ween I have not lived in vain.

Ah! could I dream when first we met,   20
When by the scanty ingle set,
Beyond the moors where curlews wheel
In Ettrick's bleakest, loneliest sheil,
Conning old songs of other times,
Most uncouth chants and crabbed rhymes;—   25
Could I e'er dream that wayward wight,
Of roguish joke, and heart so light,
In whose oft-changing eye I gazed,
Not without dread the head was crazed,

Should e'er, by genius' force alone,   30
Skim o'er an ocean sailed by none,
All the hid shoals of envy miss,
And gain such noble port as this?

    I could not: but I cherish still
Mirth at the scene, and ever will;   35
When o'er the fells we took our way,
('Tis twenty years, even to a day,
Since we two sought the fabled urn
Of marble blue by Rankleburn):
No tomb appeared; but oft we traced   40
Towns, camps, and battle-lines effaced,
Which never were, nor could remain,
Save in the bold enthusiast's brain:
The same to us,—it turned our lays
To chiefs and tales of ancient days.   45
One broken pot alone was found
Deep in the rubbish under ground,
In middle of the ancient fane,
"A gallant helmet split in twain!"
The truth was obvious; but in faith   50
On you all words were waste of breath;
You only looked demure and sly,
And sore the brow fell o'er the eye;
You could not bear that you should ride
O'er pathless waste and forest wide,   55
Only to say that you had been
To see that nought was to be seen.

    The evenings came; more social mirth
Ne'er flowed around the cottage hearth:
When Maitland's song first met your ear,   60
How the furled visage up did clear,

Beaming delight! though now a shade
Of doubt would darken into dread
That some unskilled presumptuous arm
Had marred tradition's mighty charm.   65

   Scarce grew thy lurking dread the less
Till she, the ancient Minstreless,
With fervid voice, and kindling eye,
And withered arms waving on high,
Sung forth these words in eldritch shriek,   70
While tears stood on thy nut-brown cheek—

    "Na, we are nane o' the lads o' France,
      Nor e'er pretend to be;
    We be three lads of fair Scotland,
      Auld Maitland's sons, a' three!"   75

Thy fist made all the table ring,—
"By——, Sir, but that is the thing!"

   Yes, twenty years have come and fled
Since we two met, and time has shed
His riming honours o'er each brow—   80
My state the same, how changed art thou!
But every year yet overpast
I've loved thee dearer than the last;
For all the volumes thou hast wrote,
Those that are owned, and that are not,   85
Let these be conned, even to a grain,
I've said it, and will say't again,—
Who knows thee but by these alone,
The better half is still unknown.

   I know thee well—no kinder breast   90
Beats for the woes of the distrest,

Bleeds for the wounds it cannot heal,
Or yearns more o'er thy country's weal:
Thy loves embraces Britain o'er,
And spreads and radiates with her shore;   95
Scarce fading on her ocean's foam,
But still 'tis brightest nearest home,
Till those within its central rays,
Rejoicing, bask within the blaze.

Blessed be the act of sovereign grace   100
That raised thee 'bove the rhyming race;
Blessed be the heart and head elate,
The noble generous estimate
That marked thy worth, and owned the hand
Resistless in its native land.   105
Bootless the waste of empty words,
Thy pen is worth ten thousand swords.

Long brook thy honours, gallant Knight,
So firm of soul, so staunch of right,
For had thy form but reached its prime,   110
Free from mischance in early time,
No stouter sturdier arm of weir
Had wielded sword or battle spear!
For war thy boardly frame was born,
For battle shout, and bugle-horn;   115
Thy boyish feats, thy youthful dream—
How thy muse kindles at the theme!
Chance marred the path, or Heaven's decree;
How blessed for Scotland and for me!

Scarce sounds thy name as 't did before,—   120
Walter the Abbot now no more:
Well, let it be, I'll not repine,
But love the title since 'tis thine.

Long brook thy honours, firm to stand
As Eildon rock; and that thy land,   125
The first e'er won by dint of rhyme,
May bear thy name till latest time;
And stretch from bourn of Abbot's-lea
To Philhope Cross, and Eildon Tree,
Is the heart's wish of one who's still   130
Thy grateful Shepherd of the Hill!

ALTRIVE LAKE,
April 24. 1820.

HYMN TO THE DEVIL

SPEED thee, speed thee!
Liberty lead thee!
Many this night shall hearken and heed thee.
        Far abroad,
        Demigod!   5
    What shall appal thee?
Javel, or Devil, or how shall we call thee?
Thine the night voices of joy and of weeping,
The whisper awake, and the vision when sleeping:
The bloated kings of the earth shall brood   10
On princedoms and provinces bought with blood,
Shall slubber, and snore, and to-morrow's breath
Shall order the muster and march of death:
The trumpets shall sound, and the gonfalons flee,
And thousands of souls step home to thee.   15
    Speed thee, speed thee, &c.

The warrior shall dream of battle begun,
Of field-day and foray, and foeman undone;
Of provinces sacked, and warrior store,
Of hurry and havoc, and hampers of ore;   20

Of captive maidens for joys abundant,
And ransom vast when these grow redundant.
Hurray! for the foray. Fiends ride forth a souling,
For the dogs of havock are yelping and yowling.
    Speed thee, speed thee, &c.   25

    Make the bedesman's dream
    With treasure to teem;
    To-day and to-morrow
    He has but one aim,
And 'tis still the same, and 'tis still the same.   30
But well thou knowest the sot's demerit,
His richness of flesh, and his poorness of spirit;
And well thy images thou canst frame,
On canvas of pride, with pencil of flame:
A broad demesne is a view of glory,   35
For praying a soul from purgatory:
And, O let the dame be fervent and fair,
Amorous, and righteous, and husband beware!
For there's a confession so often repeated,
The eyes are enlightened, the life-blood is heated.   40
Hish!—Hush!—soft foot and silence,
The sons of the abbot are lords of the Highlands.
Thou canst make lubbard and lighthead agree,
Wallow a while, and come home to thee.
    Speed thee, speed thee, &c.   45

Where goest thou next, by hamlet or shore,
When kings, when warriors, and priests are o'er?
These for thee have the most to do,
And these are the men must be looked unto.
On courtier deign not to look down,   50
Who swells at a smile, and faints at a frown.

With noble maid stay not to parle,
But give her one glance of the golden arle.
Then, oh, there's a creature thou needs must see,
Upright, and saintly, and stern is she!   55
'Tis the old maid, with visage demure,
With cat on her lap, and dogs on the floor.
Master, she'll prove a match for thee,
With her psalter, and crosier, and Ave Mari.
Move her with things above and below,   60
Tickle her and teaze her from lip to toe;
Should all prove vain, and nothing can move;
If dead to ambition, and cold to love,
One passion still success will crown,
A glorious energy all thine own!   65
'Tis envy; a die that never can fail
With children, matron, or maiden stale.
Shew them in dreams from night to day
A happy mother, and offspring gay;
Show them the maiden in youthful prime,   70
Followed and wooed, improving her time;
And their hearts will sicken with envy and spleen,
A leperous jaundice of yellow and green:
And though frightened for hell to a boundless degree,
They'll singe their dry perriwigs yet with thee.   75
        Speed thee, speed thee, &c.

Where goest thou next? Where wilt thou hie thee?
Still there is rubbish enough to try thee.
Whisper the matron of lordly fame,
There's a greater than she in splendor and name;   80
And her bosom shall swell with the grievous load,
And torrents of slander shall volley abroad,
Imbued with venom and bitter despair:
O sweet are the sounds to the Prince of the Air!

Reach the proud yeoman a bang with a spear,   85
And the tippling burgess a yerk on the ear;
Put fees in the eye of the poisoning leech,
And give the dull peasant a kick on the breech:
As for the flush maiden, the rosy elf,
You may pass her by, she will dream of herself.   90
But that all may be gain, and nothing loss,
Keep eye on the men with the cowl and the cross;
Then shall the world go swimming before thee,
In a full tide of liberty, licence, and glory!
  Speed thee, speed thee, &c.   95

Hail, patriot spirit! thy labours be blest!
For of all great reformers thyself wert the first;
Thou wert the first, with discernment strong,
To perceive that all rights divine were wrong;
And long hast thou spent thy sovereign breath,   100
In heaven above and in earth beneath,
And roared it from thy burning throne,
The glory of independence alone;
Proclaiming to all, with fervor and irony,
That kingly dominion's all humbug and tyranny;   105
And whoso listeth may be free,
For freedom, full freedom's the word with thee!
That life has its pleasures—the rest is a sham,
And that all comes after a flim and a flam!
   Speed thee! Speed thee!   110
   Liberty lead thee!
Many this night shall hearken and heed thee.
    Hie abroad,
    Demigod!
   Who shall defame thee?   115
King of the Elements! how shall we name thee?

RINGAN AND MAY

I HEARD a laverock singing with glee,
And oh but the bird sang cheerilye;
Then I askit at my true love Ringan,
If he kend what the bonny bird was singing?

Now, my love Ringan is blith and young, 5
But he has a fair and flattering tongue;
And oh, I'm fear'd I like ower weel
His tales of love, though kind and leal!
So I said to him, in scornful ways,
"You ken no word that wee burd says!" 10

Then my love he turn'd about to me,
And there was a smile in his pawky ee;
And he says, "My May, my dawtied dow,
I ken that strain far better nor you;
For that little fairy that lilts so loud, 15
And hangs on the fringe of the sunny cloud,
Is telling the tale, in chants and chimes,
I have told to thee a thousand times.
I will let thee hear how our strains accord,
And the laverock's sweet sang, word for word: 20

Interpretation of the Lark's Song

'OH, my love is bonny, and mild to see,
As sweetly she sits on her dewy lea,
And turns up her cheek and clear gray eye,
To list what's saying within the sky!
For she thinks my morning hymn so sweet, 25
Wi' the streamers of Heaven aneath my feet,
Where the proud goshawk could never won,
Between the gray cloud and the sun,—

And she thinks her love a thing of the skies,
Sent down from the holy Paradise,   30
To sing to the world, at morn and even,
The sweet love songs in the bowers of Heaven.

'O my love is bonny, and young, and chaste,
As sweetly she sits in her mossy nest!
And she deems the birds on bush and tree,   35
As nothing but dust and droul to me.
Though the robin warble his waesome chirl,
And the merle gar all the greenwood dirl,
And the storm-cock touts on his towering pine,
She trows their songs a mock to mine;   40
The linty's cheip a ditty tame,
And the shillfa's everlasting rhame;
The plover's whew a solo drear,
And the whilly-whaup's ane shame to hear;
And, whenever a lover comes in view,   45
She cowers beneath her screen of dew.

'O my love is bonny! her virgin breast
Is sweeter to me nor the dawning east;
And well do I like, at the gloaming still,
To dreep from the lift or the lowering hill,   50
And press her nest as white as milk,
And her breast as soft as the downy silk.' "

Now when my love Ringan had warbled away
To this base part of the laverock's lay,
My heart was like to burst in twain,   55
And the tears flow'd from mine eyne like rain;
At length he said, with a sigh full lang,
"What ails my love at the laverock's sang?"

Says I, "He's ane base and wicked bird,
   As ever rose from the dewy yird;   60
It's a shame to mount on his morning wing,
At the yetts of heaven sic sangs to sing;
And all to win, with his amorous din,
A sweet little virgin bird to sin,
And wreck, with flattery and song combined,   65
His dear little maiden's peace of mind!
Oh, were I her, I would let him see,
His songs should all be lost on me!"

Then my love took me in his arms,
And 'gan to laud my leifou charms;   70
But I would not so much as let him speak,
Nor stroke my chin, nor kiss my cheek:
For I fear'd my heart was going wrang,
It was so moved at the laverock's sang.

Yet still I lay with an upcast ee,   75
And still he was singing sae bonnilye,
That, though with my mind I had great strife,
I could not forbear it for my life,
But, as he hung on the heaven's brow,
I said, I ken not why, nor how,   80
"What's that little deevil saying now?"

Then my love Ringan, he was so glad,
He leugh till his folly pat me mad;
And he said, "My love, I will tell you true,
He seems to sing that strain to you;   85
For it says, 'I will range the yird and air
To feed my love with the finest fare;
And when she looks from her bed to me,
With the yearning love of a mother's ee,

Oh, then I will come, and draw her nearer, 90
And watch her closer, and love her dearer,
And we never shall part till our dying day,
But love and love on for ever and aye!' "

Then my heart it bled with a thrilling pleasure,
When it learn'd the laverock's closing measure, 95
And it rose, and rose, and would not rest,
And would hardly bide within my breast.
Then up I rose, and away I sprung,
And said to my love, with scornful tongue,
That it was ane big and burning shame; 100
That he and the lark were both to blame;
For there were some lays so soft and bland
That breast of maiden could not stand;
And, if he lay in the wood his lane,
Quhill I came back to list the strain 105
Of an amorous bird amang the broom,
Then he might lie quhill the day of doom!

But for all the sturt and strife I made;
For all I did, and all I said,
Alas! I fear it will be lang 110
Or I forget that wee burd's sang!
And langer still or I can flee
The lad that told that sang to me!

ST MARY OF THE LOWS

O LONE St Mary of the waves,
    In ruin lies thine ancient aisle,
While o'er thy green and lowly graves,
    The moorcocks bay, and plovers wail;

But mountain spirits on the gale   5
Oft o'er thee sound the requiem dread,
   And warriors shades, and spectres pale,
Still linger by the quiet dead.

Yes, many a chief of ancient days
   Sleeps in thy cold and hallow'd soil,   10
Hearts that would thread the forest maze,
   Alike for spousal or for spoil,
   That wist not, ween'd not, to recoil
Before the might of mortal foe,
   But thirsted for the Border broil,   15
The shout, the clang, the overthrow!

Here lies those who, o'er flood and field,
   Were hunted as the osprey's brood,
Who braved the power of man, and seal'd
   Their testimonies with their blood: 20
   But long as waves that wilder'd flood,
Their sacred memory shall be dear,
   And all the virtuous and the good
O'er their low graves shall drop the tear.

Here sleeps the last of all the race   25
   Of these old heroes of the hill,
Stern as the storm in heart and face;
   Gainsaid in faith or principle,
   Then would the fire of heaven fill
The orbit of his faded eye;   30
   Yet all within was kindness still,
Benevolence and simplicity.

GRIEVE, thou shalt hold a sacred cell
  In hearts with sin and sorrow toss'd;
While thousands, with their funeral knell,   35
  Roll down the tide of darkness, lost;
  For thou wert Truth's and Honour's boast,
Firm champion of Religion's sway!
  Who knew thee best, revered thee most,
Thou emblem of a former day!   40

Here lie old Border bowmen good;
  Ranger and stalker sleep together,
Who for the red-deer's stately brood
  Watch'd, in despite of want and weather,
  Beneath the hoary hills of heather: 45
Even Scotts, and Kerrs, and Pringles, blended
  In peaceful slumbers, rest together,
Whose fathers there to death contended.

Here lie the peaceful, simple race,
  The first old tenants of the wild,   50
Who stored the mountains of the chase
  With flocks and herds—whose manners mild
  Changed the baronial castles, piled
In every glen, into the cot,
  And the rude mountaineer beguiled,   55
Indignant, to his peaceful lot.

Here rural beauty low reposes,
  The blushing cheek, and beaming eye,
The dimpling smile, the lip of roses,
  Attractors of the burning sigh,   60
  And love's delicious pangs, that lie
Enswathed in pleasure's mellow mine:
  Maid, lover, parent, low and high,
Are mingled in thy lonely shrine.

And here lies one—here I must turn   65
    From all the noble and sublime,
And, o'er thy new but sacred urn,
    Shed the heath-flower and mountain-thyme,
    And floods of sorrow, while I chime
Above thy dust one requiem.   70
    Love was thine error, not thy crime,
Thou mildest, sweetest, mortal gem!

For ever hallow'd be thy bed,
    Beneath the dark and hoary steep;
Thy breast may flowerets overspread,   75
    And angels of the morning weep
    In sighs of heaven above thy sleep,
And tear-drops of embalming dew;
    Thy vesper hymn be from the deep,
Thy matin from the ether blue!   80

I dare not of that holy shade,
    That's pass'd away, one thought allow,
Not even a dream that might degrade
    The mercy before which I bow:
    Eternal God, what is it now?   85
Thus asks my heart: but the reply
    I aim not, wish not, to foreknow;
'Tis veil'd within eternity.

But oh, this earthly flesh and heart
    Still cling to the dear form beneath,   90
As when I saw its soul depart,
    As when I saw it calm in death:
    The dead rose and funereal wreath
Above the breast of virgin snow,
    Far lovelier than in life and breath—   95
I saw it then, and see it now.

That her fair form shall e'er decay
  One thought I may not entertain;
As she was on her dying day,
  To me she ever will remain: 100
  When Time's last shiver o'er his reign
Shall close this scene of sin and sorrow,
  How calm, how lovely, how serene,
That form shall rise upon the morrow!

Frail man! of all the arrows wounding   105
  Thy mortal heart, there is but one
Whose poison'd dart is so astounding,
  That bear it, cure it, there can none.
  It is the thought of beauty won,
To love in most supreme degree,   110
  And, by the hapless flame undone,
Cut off from nature and from thee.

THE MONITORS

THE lift looks cauldrife i' the west,
  The wan leaf wavers frae the tree,
The wind touts on the mountain's breast
  A dirge o' waesome note to me.
  It tells me that the days o' glee,   5
When summer's thrilling sweets entwined,
  An' love was blinkin' in the ee,
Are a' gane by an' far behind;

That winter wi' his joyless air,
  An' grizzely hue, is hasting nigh,   10
An' that auld age, an' carkin' care,
  In my last stage afore me lie.

Yon chill and cheerless winter sky,
Troth but 'tis eereisome to see,
   For ah! it points me to descry   15
The downfa's o' futuritye.

I daurna look unto the east,
   For there my morning shone sae sweet;
An' when I turn me to the west,
   The gloaming's like to gar me greet;   20
   The deadly hues o' snaw and sleet
Tell of a dreary onward path;
   Yon new moon on her cradle sheet,
Looks like the Hainault scythe of death.

Kind Monitors! ye tell a tale   25
   That oft has been my daily thought;
Yet, when it came, could nought avail,
   For sad experience, dearly bought,
   Tells me it was not what I ought,
But what was in my power to do,   30
   That me behoved. An' I hae fought
Against a world wi' courage true.

Yes—I hae fought an' won the day,
   Come weal, come woe, I carena by,
I am a king! My regal sway   35
   Stretches o'er Scotia's mountains high,
   And o'er the fairy vales that lie
Beneath the glimpses o' the moon,
   Or round the ledges of the sky,
In twilight's everlasting noon.   40

Who would not choose the high renown,
   'Mang Scotia's swains the chief to be,
Than be a king, an' wear a crown,
   'Mid perils, pain, an' treacherye?

Hurra! The day's my own—I'm free 45
Of statemen's guile, an' flattery's train;
   I'll blaw my reed of game an' glee,
The Shepherd is himself again!

"But, Bard—ye dinna mind your life
   Is waning down to winter snell— 50
That round your hearth young sprouts are rife,
   An' mae to care for than yoursell."
   Yes, that I do—that hearth could tell
How aft the tear-drap blinds my ee;
   What can I do, by spur or spell, 55
An' by my faith it done shall be.

And think—through poortith's eiry breach,
   Should Want approach wi' threatening brand,
I'll leave them canty sangs will reach
   From John o' Groats to Solway strand. 60
   Then what are houses, goud, or land,
To sic an heirship left in fee?
   An' I think mair o' auld Scotland,
Than to be fear'd for mine or me.

True, she has been a stepdame dour, 65
   Grudging the hard-earn'd sma' propine,
On a' my efforts looking sour,
   An' seem'd in secret to repine.
   Blest be Buccleuch an' a' his line,
For ever blessed may they be; 70
   A little hame I can ca' mine
He rear'd amid the wild for me.

Goodwife—without a' sturt or strife,
Bring ben the siller bowl wi' care;
Ye are the best an' bonniest wife, 75
   That ever fell to poet's share;

An' I'll send o'er for Frank—a pair
O' right good-heartit chiels are we—
　　We'll drink your health—an' what is mair,
We'll drink our Laird's wi' three times three.　　80

To the young Shepherd, too, we'll take
　　A rousing glass wi' right good-will;
An' the young ladies o' the Lake,
　　We'll drink in ane—an awfu' swill!
Then a' the tints o' this warld's ill　　85
　　Will vanish like the morning dew,
　　An' we'll be blithe an' blither still—
Kind winter Monitors, adieu!

This warld has mony ups an' downs,
　　Atween the cradle an' the grave,　　90
O' blithsome haun's an' broken crowns,
　　An' douks in chill misfortune's wave;
　　All these determined to outbrave,
O'er fancy's wilds I'll wing anew,
　　As lang as I can lilt a stave,—　　95
Kind winter Monitors, adieu!

SONGS

DONALD MACDONALD

I PLACE this song the first, not on account of any intrinsic merit
that it possesses,—for there it ranks rather low,—but merely because
it was my first song, and exceedingly popular when it first appeared.
I wrote it when a barefooted lad herding lambs on the Blackhouse
Heights, in utter indignation at the threatened invasion from France.
But after it had run through the Three Kingdoms, like fire set to
heather, for ten or twelve years, no one ever knew or enquired who
was the author.—It is set to the old air, "Woo'd an' married an' a'."

MY name it is Donald M'Donald,
　　I leeve in the Heelands sae grand;
I hae follow'd our banner, and will do,
　　Wherever my Maker has land.
When rankit amang the blue bonnets,　　　　　　5
　　Nae danger can fear me ava;
I ken that my brethren around me
　　Are either to conquer or fa'.
　　　　Brogues an' brochin an' a',
　　　　Brochin an' brogues an' a';　　　　　10
　　　　An' is nae her very weel aff
　　　　Wi' her brogues an' brochin an' a'?

What though we befriendit young Charlie?—
　　To tell it I dinna think shame;
Poor lad, he cam to us but barely,　　　　　　15
　　An' reckon'd our mountains his hame.

'Twas true that our reason forbade us;
  But tenderness carried the day;—
Had Geordie come friendless amang us,
  Wi' him we had a' gane away.   20
    Sword an' buckler an' a',
    Buckler an' sword an' a';
    Now for George we'll encounter the devil,
    Wi' sword an' buckler an' a'!

An' O, I wad eagerly press him   25
  The keys o' the East to retain;
For should he gie up the possession,
  We'll soon hae to force them again.
Than yield up an inch wi' dishonour,
  Though it were my finishing blow,   30
He ay may depend on M'Donald,
  Wi' his Heelanders a' in a row:
    Knees an' elbows an' a',
    Elbows an' knees an a';
    Depend upon Donald M'Donald,   35
    His knees an' elbows an' a'!

Wad Bonaparte land at Fort-William,
  Auld Europe nae langer should grane;
I laugh when I think how we'd gall him,
  Wi' bullet, wi' steel, an' wi' stane;   40
Wi' rocks o' the Nevis and Gairy
  We'd rattle him off frae our shore,
Or lull him asleep in a cairny,
  An' sing him—Lochaber no more!
    Stanes an' bullets an' a',   45
    Bullets an' stanes an' a';
    We'll finish the Corsican callan
    Wi' stanes an' bullets an' a'!

For the Gordon is good in a hurry,
    An' Campbell is steel to the bane,   50
An' Grant, an' M'Kenzie, an' Murray,
    An' Cameron will hurkle to nane;
The Stuart is sturdy an' loyal,
    An' sae is M'Leod an' M'Kay;
An' I, their gudebrither, M'Donald,   55
    Shall ne'er be the last in the fray!
      Brogues an' brochin an' a',
      Brochin an' brogues an' a';
      An' up wi' the bonny blue bonnet,
      The kilt an' the feather an' a'!*   60

* I once heard the above song sung in the theatre at Lancaster, when
the singer substituted the following lines of his own for the last verse:

    "For Jock Bull he is good in a hurry,
      An' Sawney is steel to the bane,
    An' wee Davie Welsh is a widdy,
      An' Paddy will hurkle to nane;
    They'll a' prove baith sturdy and loyal,
      Come dangers around them what may,
    An' I, their gudebrither, M'Donald,
      Shall ne'er be the last in the fray !" &c.

It took exceedingly well, and was three times encored, and there was I
sitting in the gallery, applauding as much as any body. My vanity prompted
me to tell a jolly Yorkshire manufacturer that night, that I was the author
of the song. He laughed excessively at my assumption, and told the land-
lady that he took me for a half-crazed Scots pedlar.

Another anecdote concerning this song I may mention; and I do it with
no little pride, as it is a proof of the popularity of Donald M'Donald among
a class, to inspire whom with devotion to the cause of their country was
at the time a matter of no little consequence. Happening upon one occasion
to be in a wood in Dumfries-shire, through which wood the highroad passed,
I heard a voice singing; and a turn of the road soon brought in sight a
soldier, who seemed to be either travelling home upon furlough, or return-
ing to his regiment. When the singer approached nearer, I distinguished
the notes of my own song of Donald M'Donald. As the lad proceeded with
his song, he got more and more into the spirit of the thing, and on coming
to the end,

    "An' up wi' the bonny blue bonnet,
      The kilt an' the feather an' a'!"

in the height of his enthusiasm, he hoisted his cap on the end of his staff,
and danced it about triumphantly. I stood ensconced behind a tree, and
heard and saw all without being observed.

BONNY PRINCE CHARLIE

I s it not singular how this song should have been so popular ? There can be no dispute that it is one of my worst. The air was likewise given me by my friend the late Mr Niel Gow, and to it I dashed down the words at random. Afterwards, when there was like to be a dust among the music-sellers about the tune, Mr Robertson wrote to me about it, and to justify his appropriation, assured me that the air was that of "Gala Water!" I answered that I would not dispute his authority, but after that, no man was entitled to disbelieve that a horsehair would turn an eel.—For the music of this and the foregoing song [i.e. *Flora MacDonald's Lament.—Ed.*], the best sets are to be found in Mr Purdie's Border Garland, by Dewar.

CAM ye by Athol, lad wi' the philabeg,
Down by the Tummel, or banks o' the Garry,
Saw ye our lads, wi' their bonnets and white cockades,
Leaving their mountains to follow Prince Charlie ?
   Follow thee! follow thee! wha wadna follow thee ? 5
   Lang hast thou loved and trusted us fairly!
   Charlie, Charlie, wha wadna follow thee,
   King o' the Highland hearts, bonny Prince Charlie ?

I hae but ae son, my gallant young Donald;
But if I had ten, they should follow Glengarry!   10
Health to M'Donnell and gallant Clan-Ronald,
For these are the men that will die for their Charlie!
   Follow thee! follow thee! &c.

I'll to Lochiel and Appin, and kneel to them,
Down by Lord Murray, and Roy of Kildarlie;   15
Brave M'Intosh he shall fly to the field with them;
These are the lads I can trust wi' my Charlie!
   Follow thee! follow thee! &c.

Down through the Lowlands, down wi' the Whigamore!
Loyal true Highlanders, down wi' them rarely!   20
Ronald an' Donald, drive on, wi' the broad claymore,
Over the necks of the foes o' Prince Charlie!

Follow thee! follow thee! wha wadna follow thee?
Lang hast thou loved and trusted us fairly!
Charlie, Charlie, wha wadna follow thee, 25
King o' the Highland hearts, bonny Prince Charlie?

THE SKYLARK

A little pastoral song, worth half-a-dozen of the foregoing.—For
the fine original air, see Mr Purdie's Border Garland.

BIRD of the wilderness,
Blithesome and cumberless,
Sweet be thy matin o'er moorland and lea!
Emblem of happiness,
Blest is thy dwelling-place— 5
O to abide in the desert with the!
Wild is thy lay and loud,
Far in the downy cloud,
Love gives it energy, love gave it birth.
Where, on thy dewy wing, 10
Where art thou journeying?
Thy lay is in heaven, thy love is on earth.

O'er fell and fountain sheen,
O'er moor and mountain green,
O'er the red streamer that heralds the day, 15
Over the cloudlet dim,
Over the rainbow's rim,
Musical cherub, soar, singing, away!
Then, when the gloaming comes,
Low in the heather blooms 20
Sweet will thy welcome and bed of love be!
Emblem of happiness,
Blest is thy dwelling-place—
O to abide in the desert with thee!

THE NOCTES SANG

Was made one day in Edinburgh, for singing in Ambrose's at night, [i.e. the Ambrose's of the *Noctes Ambrosianae.—Ed.*] on a particular occasion, when a number of foreign literary gentlemen were to be of the party. I did not sing it till late at night, when we were all beginning to get merry; and the effect on the party was like electricity. It was encored I know not how oft, and Mr Gillies ruffed and screamed out so loud in approbation, that he fell from his chair, and brought an American gentleman down with him. I have lost a verse of it, but it is likely to have been preserved in the Noctes Ambrosianæ. It has been always the first song at our jovial meetings ever since. The air is my own, and a very capital one. I believe it is preserved in the Noctes and nowhere else. [The lost verse mentioned by Hogg is restored in the present edition.—*Ed.*]

If e'er you wad be a brave fellow, young man,
Beware o' the Blue an' the Yellow, young man;
    For if ye wad be strang,
    An' wad wish to live lang,
Come join wi' the lads that get mellow, young man!   5

Like the crack of a squib that is thrawn on, young man,
Compared wi' the roar of a cannon, young man,
    Sae is a Whig's blow
    To the pith that's below
The brand of auld Geordie Buchanan, young man.   10

I heard a bit burd in the braken, young man,
It sung till the Whigs were a' quakin', young man;
    An' aye the sad lay
    Was, Alack for the day!
For the Blue an' the Yellow's forsaken, young man!   15
The day is arriv'd that's nae joking, young man;
'Tis vain to be murmuring and mocking, young man:
    A Whig may be leal,
    But he'll never fight weel,
As lang as he dadds wi' a docken, young man.   20

O wha wadna laugh at their capers, young man?
Like auld maidens, fash'd wi' the vapours, young man,
    We have turned them adrift
    To their very last shift,
That's—*puffing the Radical Papers, young man.*   25
If ye wad hear tell o' their pingle, young man,
Gae list that wee burd in the dingle, young man;
    Its notes o' despair
    Are sae loud in the air,
That the windows of heaven play jingle, young man!   30

I'll gie you a toast of the auldest, young man,
The loyal heart ne'er was the cauldest, young man;
    Our King an' his Throne,
    Be his glory our own,
An' the last o' his days aye the bauldest, young man!   35
But as for the rogue that wad hector, young man,
And set us at odds wi' a lecture,* young man,
    May he dance Cutty-mun,†
    Wi' his neb to the sun,
An' his doup to the General Director,‡ young man!   40

* A celebrated London professor was lecturing here then.
† *Cutty-mun*; an old Scottish tune of exceedingly quick and cramp time.
‡ This is a mysterious allusion to the common place of execution in Edinburgh. C. N. *Blackwood's Magazine.* [C. N. signifies Christopher North. -*Ed.*]

O, JEANIE, THERE'S NAETHING
TO FEAR YE!

Happening to spend an evening, as I had done many, with Patrick
Maxwell, Esq., he played the old air, "Over the Border," so well, that
I could get no rest or sleep till I had composed the following verses
for it that I could croon to myself. The late Mrs Gray went over and
corrected them next day. It has been by far the most popular love-
song I ever wrote.—For the air, see The Border Garland.

O, MY lassie, our joy to complete again,
   Meet me again i' the gloaming, my dearie;
Low down in the dell let us meet again—
   O, Jeanie, there's naething to fear ye!
Come, when the wee bat flits silent and eiry, 5
Come, when the pale face o' Nature looks weary;
     Love be thy sure defence,
     Beauty and innocence—
O, Jeanie, there's naething to fear ye!

Sweetly blows the haw an' the rowan-tree, 10
   Wild roses speck our thicket sae breery;
Still, still will our walk in the greenwood be—
   O, Jeanie, there's naething to fear ye!
List when the blackbird o' singing grows weary,
List when the beetle-bee's bugle comes near ye, 15
     Then come with fairy haste,
     Light foot, an' beating breast—
O, Jeanie, there's naething to fear ye!

Far, far will the bogle an' brownie be,
   Beauty an' truth, they darena come near it; 20
Kind love is the tie of our unity,
   A' maun love it, an' a' maun revere it.

'Tis love makes the sang o' the woodland sae cheery,
Love gars a' nature look bonny that's near ye;
    That makes the rose sae sweet,   25
    Cowslip an' violet—
O, Jeanie, there's naething to fear ye!

THE VILLAGE OF BALMAQUHAPPLE

NORTH

Stop, stop, Beelzebub, and read aloud that bit of
paper you have in your fist.

BEELZEBUB

Yes, sir.

SHEPHERD

Lord sauf us, what a voice! They're my ain verses,
too. Whisht, whisht!

BEELZEBUB *sings "The Great Muckle Village of Bal-*
maquhapple," to the tune of "The Sodger Laddie."

D'YE ken the big village of Balmaquhapple,
The great muckle village of Balmaquhapple?
'Tis steep'd in iniquity up to the thrapple,
An' what's to become o' poor Balmaquhapple?
Fling a' aff your bannets, an' kneel for your life, fo'ks, 5
And pray to St Andrew, the god o' the Fife fo'ks;
Gar a' the hills yout wi' sheer vociferation,
And thus you may cry on sic needfu' occasion:

"O, blessed St Andrew, if e'er ye could pity fo'k,
Men fo'k or women fo'k, country or city fo'k,   10
Come for this aince wi' the auld thief to grapple,
An' save the great village of Balmaquhapple

Frae drinking an' leeing, an' flyting an' swearing,
An' sins that ye wad be affrontit at hearing,
An' cheating an' stealing; O, grant them redemption,   15
All save an' except the few after to mention:

"There's Johnny the elder, wha hopes ne'er to need ye
Sae pawkie, sae holy, sae gruff, an' sae greedy;
Wha prays every hour as the wayfarer passes,
But aye at a hole where he watches the lasses;   20
He's cheated a thousand, an' e'en to this day yet,
Can cheat a young lass, or they're leears that say it;
Then gie him his gate; he's sae slee an' sae civil,
Perhaps in the end he may wheedle the devil.

"There's Cappie the cobbler, an' Tammie the tinman,   25
An Dickie the brewer, an' Peter the skinman,
An' Geordie our deacon, for want of a better,
An' Bess, wha delights in the sins that beset her.
O, worthy St Andrew, we canna compel ye,
But ye ken as weel as a body can tell ye,   30
If these gang to heaven, we'll a' be sae shockit,
Your garret o' blue will but thinly be stockit.

"But for a' the rest, for the women's sake, save them,
Their bodies at least, an' their sauls, if they have them;
But it puzzles Jock Lesly, an' sma' it avails,   35
If they dwell in their stamocks, their heads, or their tails.
An' save, without word of confession auricular,
The clerk's bonny daughters, an' Bell in particular;
For ye ken that their beauty's the pride an' the staple
Of the great wicked village of Balmaquhapple!"   40

NORTH (*aside to* TICKLER)

Hogg's, bad.

SHEPHERD

What's that you twa are speaking about? Speak up!

NORTH

These fine lines must be preserved, James. Pray, are they allegorical?

SHEPHERD

Preserve's, what a dracht's in that lum! &c.—

Noctes Ambrosianæ, No. XXVI.

Christopher might well ask such a question, for I cannot conceive what could induce me to write a song like this. It must undoubtedly have some allusion to circumstances which I have quite forgot.

WHEN THE KYE COMES HAME

In the title and chorus of this favourite pastoral song, I choose rather to violate a rule in grammar, than a Scottish phrase so common, that when it is altered into the proper way, every shepherd and shepherd's sweetheart account it nonsense. I was once singing it at a wedding with great glee the latter way, ("when the kye come hame,") when a tailor, scratching his head, said, "It was a terrible affectit way that!" I stood corrected, and have never sung it so again. It is to the old air of " Shame fa' the gear and the blathrie o't," with an additional chorus. It is set to music in the Noctes, at which it was first sung, and in no other place that I am aware of.

> COME all ye jolly shepherds
>   That whistle through the glen,
> I'll tell ye of a secret
>   That courtiers dinna ken:
> What is the greatest bliss   5
>   That the tongue o' man can name?
> 'Tis to woo a bonny lassie
>   When the kye comes hame.

When the kye comes hame,
  When the kye come hame,   10
'Tween the gloaming and the mirk,
  When the kye come hame.

'Tis not beneath the coronet,
  Nor canopy of state,
'Tis not on couch of velvet,   15
  Nor arbour of the great—
'Tis beneath the spreading birk,
  In the glen without the name,
Wi' a bonny, bonny lassie,
  When the kye comes hame.   20
    When the kye comes hame, &c.

There the blackbird bigs his nest
  For the mate he loes to see,
And on the topmost bough,
  O, a happy bird is he;   25
Where he pours his melting ditty,
  And love is a' the theme,
And he'll woo his bonny lassie
  When the kye comes hame.
    When the kye comes hame, &c.   30

When the blewart bears a pearl,
  And the daisy turns a pea,
And the bonny lucken gowan
  Has fauldit up her ee,
Then the laverock frae the blue lift   35
  Doops down, an' thinks nae shame
To woo his bonny lassie
  When the kye comes hame.
    When the kye come hame, &c.

See yonder pawkie shepherd,   40
   That lingers on the hill,
His ewes are in the fauld,
   An' his lambs are lying still;
Yet he downa gang to bed,
   For his heart is in a flame,   45
To meet his bonny lassie
   When the kye comes hame.
     When the kye comes hame, &c.

When the little wee bit heart
   Rises high in the breast,   50
An' the little wee bit starn
   Rises red in the east,
O there's a joy sae dear,
   That the heart can hardly frame,
Wi' a bonny, bonny lassie,   55
   When the kye comes hame!
     When the kye comes hame, &c.

Then since all nature joins
   In this love without alloy,
O, wha wad prove a traitor   60
   To Nature's dearest joy?
Or wha wad choose a crown,
   Wi' its perils and its fame,
And *miss* his bonny lassie
   When the kye comes hame?   65
    When the kye comes hame,
    When the kye comes hame,
  'Tween the gloaming and the mirk,
    When the kye comes hame!

I composed the foregoing song I neither know how nor when; for when the "Three Perils of Man" came first to my hand, and I saw this song put into the mouth of a drunken poet, and mangled in the singing, I had no recollection of it wherever. I had written it off hand along with the prose, and quite forgot it. But I liked it, altered it, and it has been my favourite pastoral for singing ever since. It is too long to be sung from beginning to end; but only the second and antepenult verses can possibly be dispensed with, and these not very well neither.

M'LEAN'S WELCOME

I versified this song at Meggernie Castle, in Glen-Lyon, from a scrap of prose said to be the translation, *verbatim*, of a Gaelic song, and to a Gaelic air, sung by one of the sweetest singers and most accomplished and angelic beings of the human race. But, alas! earthly happiness is not always the lot of those who, in our erring estimation, most deserve it. She is now no more, and many a strain have I poured to her memory. The air is arranged by Smith.—See the Scottish Minstrel.

COME o'er the stream, Charlie,
Dear Charlie, brave Charlie;
Come o'er the stream, Charlie,
   And dine with M'Lean;
And though you be weary, 5
We'll make your heart cheery,
And welcome our Charlie,
   And his loyal train.
We'll bring down the track deer,
We'll bring down the black steer, 10
The lamb from the braken,
   And doe from the glen,
The salt sea we'll harry,
And bring to our Charlie
The cream from the bothy 15
   And curd from the pen.

Come o'er the stream, Charlie,
Dear Charlie, brave Charlie;
Come o'er the sea, Charlie,
 And dine with M'Lean;   20
And you shall drink freely
The dews of Glen-sheerly,
That stream in the starlight
 When kings do not ken,
And deep be your meed   25
Of the wine that is red,
To drink to your sire,
 And his friend the M'Lean.

Come o'er the stream, Charlie,
Dear Charlie, brave Charlie;   30
Come o'er the stream, Charlie,
 And dine with M'Lean;
If aught will invite you,
Or more will delight you,
'Tis ready, a troop of our bold Highlandmen,   35
 All ranged on the heather,
 With bonnet and feather,
Strong arms and broad claymores,
 Three hundred and ten!

WHEN MAGGY GANGS AWAY

A very different strain from the foregoing [i.e. *The Harp of Ossian.—Ed.*]. I heard a girl lilting over the first line to my little daughter Maggy, and forthwith went in and made a song of it.—It is set to a lively old strain by Bishop, and is beginning to be a favourite.

 O WHAT will a' the lads do
  When Maggy gangs away?
 O what will a' the lads do
  When Maggy gangs away?

There's no a heart in a' the glen   5
  That disna dread the day.
O what will a' the lads do
  When Maggy gangs away?

Young Jock has ta'en the hill for't—
  A waefu' wight is he;   10
Poor Harry's ta'en the bed for't,
  An' laid him down to dee;
An' Sandy's gane unto the kirk,
  And learnin' fast to pray.
And, O, what will the lads do   15
  When Maggy gangs away?

The young laird o' the Lang-Shaw
  Has drunk her health in wine;
The priest has said—in confidence—
  The lassie was divine—   20
And that is mair in maiden's praise
  Than ony priest should say:
But, O, what will the lads do
  When Maggy gangs away?

The wailing in our green glen   25
  That day will quaver high,
'Twill draw the redbreast frae the wood,
  The laverock frae the sky;
The fairies frae their beds o' dew
  Will rise an' join the lay: 30
An' hey! what a day will be
  When Maggy gangs away!

DONALD M'GILLAVRY

Was originally published in the Jacobite Relics, without any notice of its being an original composition; an omission which entrapped the Edinburgh Review into a high but unintentional compliment to the author. After reviewing the Relics in a style of most determined animosity, and protesting over and over again that I was devoid of all taste and discrimination, the tirade concluded in these terms: "That we may not close this article without a specimen of the good songs which the book contains, we shall select the one which, for sly, characteristic Scotch humour, seems to us the best, though we doubt if any of our English readers will relish it." The opportunity of retaliating upon the reviewer's want of sagacity was too tempting to be lost; and the authorship of the song was immediately avowed in a letter to the Editor of Blackwood's Magazine. "After all," said this avowal, "between ourselves, Donald M'Gillavry, which he has selected as the best specimen of the true old Jacobite song, and as remarkably above its fellows for 'sly, characteristic Scotch humour,' is no other than a trifle of my own, which I put in to fill up a page!"

I cannot help remarking here, that the Edinburgh Review seems to be at fault in a melancholy manner wherever it comes to speak of Scottish songs. My friend Mr William Laidlaw's song of Lucy's Flitting appeared first in the Forest Minstrel, and immediately became popular throughout Scotland. It was inserted in every future selection of Scottish songs, and of course found a place in Allan Cunningham's collection. Here it is to be supposed the Edinburgh reviewer saw and heard of it for the first time; and, with some words of praise, he most condescendingly introduced it to public notice, after it had been sung and appreciated from the cottage to the palace for a space of nearly twenty years. This reminds me of an old gentleman, who, as he said, "always liked to have people known to each other;" so one day he made a party for the purpose of introducing two cousins who had been brought up under the same roof. The company took the matter with gravity, and the joke passed off very well at the old gentleman's expense.—For the air, see Jacobite Relics, vol. i.

DONALD's gane up the hill hard an' hungry,
Donald's come down the hill wild an' angry;
Donald will clear the gouk's nest cleverly;
Here's to the king an' Donald M'Gillavry!

Come like a weigh-bauk, Donald M'Gillavry,   5
Come like a weigh-bauk, Donald M'Gillavry;
Balance them fair, an' balance them cleverly,
Off wi' the counterfeit, Donald M'Gillavry!

Donald's come o'er the hill trailin' his tether, man,
As he war wud, or stang'd wi' an ether, man;   10
When he gaes back, there's some will look merrily;
Here's to King James an' Donald M'Gillavry!
Come like a weaver, Donald M'Gillavry,
Come like a weaver, Donald M'Gillavry;
Pack on your back an elwand o' steelary,   15
Gie them full measure, my Donald M'Gillavry!

Donald has foughten wi' reif and roguery,
Donald has dinner'd wi' banes an' beggary;
Better it war for whigs an' whiggery
Meeting the deevil than Donald M'Gillavry.   20
Come like a tailor, Donald M'Gillavry,
Come like a tailor, Donald M'Gillavry;
Push about, in an' out, thimble them cleverly—
Here's to King James an' Donald M'Gillavry!

Donald's the callant that bruiks nae tangleness,   25
Whigging an' prigging an' a' newfangleness;
They maun be gane, he winna be baukit, man;
He maun hae justice, or rarely he'll tak it, man.
Come like a cobler, Donald M'Gillavry,
Come like a cobler, Donald M'Gillavry;   30
Bore them, an' yerk them, an' lingel them cleverly—
Up wi' King James an' Donald M'Gillavry!

Donald was mumpit wi' mirds and mockery,
Donald was blindit wi' bladds o' property;
Arles ran high, but makings war naething, man;   35
Gudeness, how Donald is flyting an' fretting, man!

Come like the deevil, Donald M'Gillavry,
Come like the deevil, Donald M'Gillavry;
Skelp them an' scadd them pruved sae unbritherly—
Up wi' King James an' Donald M'Gillavry!   40

CHARLIE IS MY DARLING

Altered from the original, at the request of a lady who sung it sweetly
—and published in the Jacobite Relics.

'TWAS on a Monday morning,
   Right early in the year,
That Charlie came to our town,
   The Young Chevalier.
     An' Charlie is my darling,   5
       My darling, my darling,
     Charlie is my darling,
       The Young Chevalier.

As Charlie he came up the gate,
   His face shone like the day;   10
I grat to see the lad come back
   That had been lang away.
     An' Charlie is my darling, &c.

Then ilka bonny lassie sang,
   As to the door she ran,   15
Our king shall hae his ain again,
   An' Charlie is the man:
     For Charlie he's my darling, &c.

Outower you moory mountain,
   An' down the craigy glen,   20
Of naething else our lasses sing
   But Charlie an' his men.
     An' Charlie he's my darling, &c.

Our Highland hearts are true an' leal,
   An' glow without a stain;   25
Our Highland swords are metal keen,
   An' Charlie he's our ain.
     An' Charlie he's my darling,
      My darling, my darling;
     Charlie he's my darling,   30
      The young Chevalier.

MEG O' MARLEY

NORTH

You were once so good as to flatter me, by saying that I ought to go into Parliament. Now, James, if you wish it, I'll bring you in.

SHEPHERD

I haena the least ambition. Sae far frae envying the glory o' the orators i' that house, I wadna swap ane o' my ain wee bits o' sangs wi' the langest-windit speech that has been "Hear! hear'd!" this session.

TICKLER

James, let us have Meg o' Marley.

SHEPHERD (*sings*)

O KEN ye Meg o' Marley glen,
   The bonny blue-eed dearie?
She's play'd the deil amang the men,
   An' a' the land's grown eery;
She's stown the "Bangor" frae the clerk,   5
   An' snool'd him wi' the shame o't;
The minister's fa'n through the text,
   An' Meg gets a' the blame o't.

The ploughman ploughs without the sock;
   The gadman whistles sparely;   10
The shepherd pines amang his flock,
   An' turns his een to Marley;
The tailor lad's fa'n ower the bed;
   The cobler ca's a parley;
The weaver's neb's out through the web,   15
   An' a' for Meg o' Marley.

What's to be done, for our gudeman
   Is flyting late an' early?
He rises but to curse an' ban,
   An' sits down but to ferly.   20
But ne'er had love a brighter lowe
   Than light his torches sparely
At the bright een an' blithesome brow
   O' bonny Meg o' Marley.

NORTH

   A simple matter, but well worth Joseph Hume's four
hours' speech, and forty-seven resolutions.—

NOCTES AMBROSIANÆ, NO. XXV

BLACK MARY

Was set by young Gow to a fine Gaelic air, called "Is fallain gun dith
thainig thu;" but I have forgot where it is to be found. My songs, bad
as many of them are, have been for these last thirty years published
in newspapers and other periodicals over all Britain, and there is
only one person alive who ever can collect them, Mr John Aitken,
of the house of Constable and Co.

   MARY is my only joy,
   Mary is blithe, and Mary is coy,
   Mary's the goud where there's nae alloy—
      Though black, yet O she's bonny!

Her breath is the birken bower o' spring,   5
Her lips the young rose opening,
An' her hair is the hue o' the raven's wing,
　　She's black, but O she's bonny!

The star that gilds the e'ening sky,
Though bright its ray, may never vie   10
Wi' Mary's dark and liquid eye—
　　Though black, yet O she's bonny!
In you green wood there is a bower,
Where lies a bed of witching power;
Under that bed there blooms a flower,   15
　　That steals the heart unwary.

O, there is a charm, and there is a spell,
That, O an' alack! I know too well;
A pang that the tongue may hardly tell,
　　Though felt baith late an' early.   20
The beauteous flower beneath the tree,
The spell o' the wildest witcherye,
The goud an' the gear an' a' to me
　　Is my black but bonny Mary!

LOVE IS LIKE A DIZZINESS

The following ridiculous song, which was written twenty-six years
ago, has been so long a favourite with the country lads and lasses,
that for their sakes I insert it, knowing very well they would be much
disappointed at missing it out of this volume.—It is to the Irish air
called "Paddy's Wedding."

　　　　I LATELY lived in quiet case,
　　　　　　An' never wish'd to marry, O!
　　　　But when I saw my Peggy's face,
　　　　　　I felt a sad quandary, O!

Though wild as only Athol deer,   5
  She has trepann'd me fairly, O!
Her cherry cheeks an' een sae clear
  Torment me late an' early, O!
    O, love, love, love!
      Love is like a dizziness;   10
    It winna let a poor body
    Gang about his biziness!

To tell my feats this single week
  Wad mak a daft-like diary, O!
I drave my cart outow'r a dike,   15
  My horses in a miry, O!
I wear my stockings white an' blue,
  My love's sae fierce an' fiery, O!
I drill the land that I should plough,
  An' plough the drills entirely, O!   20
    O, love, love, love! &c.

Ae morning, by the dawn o' day,
  I rase to theek the stable, O!
I keust my coat, an' plied away
  As fast as I was able, O!   25
I wrought that morning out an' out,
  As I'd been redding fire, O!
When I had done an' look'd about,
  Gudefaith, it was the byre, O!
    O, love, love, love! &c.   30

Her wily glance I'll ne'er forget,
  The dear, the lovely blinkin o't
Has pierced me through an' through the heart,
  An' plagues me wi' the prinkling o't.

I tried to sing, I tried to pray,   35
    I tried to drown't wi' drinkin' o't,
I tried wi' sport to drive't away,
    But ne'er can sleep for thinkin o't.
O, love, love, love! &c.

Nae man can tell what pains I prove,   40
    Or how severe my pliskie, O!
I swear I'm sairer drunk wi' love
    Than ever I was wi' whisky, O!
For love has raked me fore an' aft,
    I scarce can lift a leggie, O!   45
I first grew dizzy, then gaed daft,
    An' soon I'll dee for Peggy, O!
O, love, love, love!
    Love is like a dizziness
It winna let a poor body   50
    Gang about his biziness!

A WITCH'S CHANT

This is a most unearthly song, copied from an unearthly tragedy of my own, published anonymously with others, in two volumes, in 1817, by Messrs Longman and Co., and John Ballantyne. The title of the play is All-Hallow Eve. It was suggested to me by old Henry Mackenzie, after a short but intimate acquaintance. I threw it aside, and my eyes never fell upon it till this night, the last of November, 1830. The poetry of the play has astounded me. The following is but a flea-bite to some of it. [The punctuation of the above note in the original seems to be mistaken, and it has been altered. The original reads:'. . . Henry Mackenzie. After a short but intimate acquaintance, I . . .'.—*Ed.*]

THOU art weary, weary, weary,
    Thou art weary and far away,
Hear me, gentle spirit, hear me,
    Come before the dawn of day.

I hear a small voice from the hill,   5
The vapour is deadly, pale, and still—
A murmuring sough is on the wood,
And the witching star is red as blood.

And in the cleft of heaven I scan
The giant form of a naked man,   10
His eye is like the burning brand,
And he holds a sword in his right hand.

All is not well. By dint of spell,
Somewhere between the heaven and hell
There is this night a wild deray,   15
The spirits have wander'd from their way.

The purple drops shall tinge the moon
As she wanders through the midnight noon;
And the dawning heaven shall all be red
With blood by guilty angels shed.   20

Be as it will, I have the skill
To work by good or work by ill;
Then here's for pain, and here's for thrall,
And here's for conscience, worst of all.

Another chant, and then, and then,   25
Spirits shall come or Christian men—
Come from the earth, the air, or the sea,
Great Gil-Moules, I cry to thee!

Sleep'st thou, wakest thou, lord of the wind,
Mount thy steeds and gallop them blind;   30
And the long-tailed fiery dragon outfly,
The rocket of heaven, the bomb of the sky.

Over the dog-star, over the wain,
Over the cloud, and the rainbow's mane,
Over the mountain, and over the sea,   35
   Haste—haste—haste to me!

Then here's for trouble, and here's for smart,
And here's for the pang that seeks the heart;
Here's for madness, and here's for thrall,
And here's for conscience, the worst of all!   40

AULD ETTRICK JOHN

This, and the four songs that follow [i.e. 'Doctor Monroe', 'Sing on, sing on, my Bonny Bird', 'Jock an' his Mother', and 'On Ettrick Clear'.—*Ed.*], are all compositions of my early youth, made for the sphere around the cottage hearth and the farmer's kitchen-ingle, without the most distant prospect of any higher distinction. Therefore, with all the hankerings of early youth, even in my own estimation they are below par in poetical merit, and ought not to have been here. But they have been such general favourites among the class for which they were framed, for the last thirty years, that to them the leaving out of these songs would make a petrifying blank; it would be like a parent denying the first of his offspring. For the sakes, therefore, of the shepherds, cottagers, and rosy servant maids, these homely songs are preserved, while scores of more polished ones are left out; for nothing can be more satiating than a whole volume of songs all of the same grade.

THERE dwalt a man on Ettrick side,
   An honest man I wat was he,
His name was John, an' he was born
   A year afore the thretty-three.
He wed a wife when he was young,   5
   But she had dee'd, and John was wae;
He wantit lang, at length did gang
   To court Nell Brunton o' the Brae.

Auld John cam daddin' down the hill,
   His arm was waggin' manfullye,   10
He thought his shadow look'd nae ill,
   As aft he keek'd aside to see;
His shoon war four punds weight a-piece,
   On ilka leg a ho had he,
His doublet strang was large an' lang,   15
   His breeks they hardly reach'd his knee;

His coat was thread about wi' green,
   The moths had wrought it muckle harm,
The pouches war an ell atween,
   The cuff was fauldit up the arm;   20
He wore a bonnet on his head,
   The bung upon his shoulders lay,
An' by its neb ye wad hae read
   That Johnnie view'd the milky way:

For Johnnie to himsell he said,   25
   As he came duntin' down the brae,
"A wooer ne'er should hing his head,
   But blink the breeze an' brow the day;"
An' Johnnie said unto himsell,
   "A wooer risks nae broken banes;   30
I'll tell the lassie sic a tale
   Will gar her look twa gates at anes."

But yet, for a' his antic dress,
   His cheeks wi' healthy red did glow;
His joints war knit and firm like brass,   35
   Though siller-grey his head did grow.
An' John, although he had nae lands,
   Had twa gude kie amang the knowes;
A hunder punds in honest hands,
   An' sax-an-thretty doddit yowes.   40

An' Nelly was a sonsy lass,
   Fu' ripe an' ruddy was her mou',
Her een war like twa beads o' glass,
   Her brow was white like Cheviot woo;
Her cheeks were bright as heather-bells,   45
   Her bosom like December snaw,
Her teeth war whiter nor egg-shells,
   Her hair was like the hoody craw.

John crackit o' his bob-tail'd yowes;
   He crackit o' his good milk-kie,   50
His kebbucks, hams, an' cogs o' brose,
   An' siller out at trust forby;
An' aye he show'd his boordly limb,
   As bragging o' his feats sae rare,
An' a' the honours paid to him   55
   At kirk, at market, or at fair.

Wi' sicklike say he wan the day,
   Nell soon became his dashin' bride;
But ilka joy soon fled away
   Frae Johnnie's canty ingle side;   60
For there was fretting late an' air,
   An' something aye a-wanting still,
The saucy taunt an' bitter jeer—
   Now, sic a life does unco ill.

An' John will be a gaishen soon;   65
   His teeth are frae their sockets flown;
The hair's peel'd aff his head aboon;
   His face is milk-an'-water grown;
His legs, that firm like pillars stood,
   Are now grown toom an' unco sma';   70
She's reaved him sair o' flesh an' blood,
   An' peace o' mind, the warst of a'.

May ilka lassie understand
   In time the duties of a wife;
But youth wi' youth gae hand in hand,   75
   Or time the sweetest joys o' life.
Ye men whase heads are turning grey,
   Wha to the grave are hastin' on,
Let reason a' your passions sway,
   An' mind the fate o' Ettrick John.   80

Ye lasses, lightsome, blithe, an' fair,
   Let pure affection win the hand;
Ne'er stoop to lead a life o' care
   Wi' doited age, for gear or land.
When ilka lad your beauty slights,   85
   An' ilka blush is broke wi' wae,
Ye'll mind the lang an' lanesome nights
   O' Nell, the lassie o' the Brae.

DOCTOR MONROE

"Dear Doctor, be clever, an' fling aff your beaver,
   Come, bleed me an' blister me, dinna be slow;
I'm sick, I'm exhausted, my prospects are blasted,
   An' a' driven heels o'er head, Doctor Monroe!"
"Be patient, dear fellow, you foster your fever;   5
   Pray, what's the misfortune that troubles you so?"
"O, Doctor! I'm ruin'd, I'm ruin'd for ever—
   My lass has foresaken me, Doctor Monroe!

"I meant to have married, an' tasted the pleasures,
   The sweets, the enjoyments from wedlock that flow;   10
But she's ta'en another, an' broken my measures,
   An' fairly dumfounder'd me, Doctor Monroe!

I am fool'd, I am dover'd as dead as a herring—
　　Good sir, you're a man of compassion, I know;
Come, bleed me to death, then, unflinching, unerring,　　15
　　Or grant me some poison, dear Doctor Monroe!"

The Doctor he flang aff his big-coat an' beaver,
　　He took out his lance, an' he sharpen'd it so;
No judge ever look'd more decided or graver—
　　"I've oft done the same, sir," says Doctor Monroe,　　20
"For gamblers, rogues, jockeys, and desperate lovers,
　　But I always make charge of a hundred, or so."
The patient look'd pale, and cried out in shrill
　　　　quavers,
　　"The devil! do you say so, sir, Doctor Monroe?"

"O yes, sir, I'm sorry there's nothing more common;　　25
　　I like it—it pays—but, ere that length I go,
A man that goes mad for the love of a woman
　　I sometimes can cure with a lecture, or so."
"Why, thank you, sir; there spoke the man and the
　　　　friend too;
　　Death is the last reckoner with friend or with foe,　　30
The lecture then, first, if you please, I'll attend to;
　　The other, of course, you know, Doctor Monroe."

The lecture is said—How severe, keen, an' cutting,
　　Of love an' of wedlock, each loss an' each woe,
The patient got up—o'er the floor he went strutting,　　35
　　Smiled, caper'd, an' shook hands with Doctor
　　　　Monroe.
He dresses, an' flaunts it with Bell, Sue, an' Chirsty,
　　But freedom an' fun chooses not to forego;
He still lives a bachelor, drinks when he's thirsty,
　　An' sings like a lark, an' loves Doctor Monroe!　　40

ATHOL CUMMERS

[In the 1831 *Songs*, 'Athol Cummers' follows the four songs mentioned in Hogg's note on **'Auld Ettrick John'**.—*Ed.*]

I must add one other of the same quality, for two, with me, potent reasons.

1st, The song was composed at the request of a beloved parent. I remember it well. One evening in the winter of 1800, I was sawing away on the fiddle with great energy and elevation, and having executed the strathspey called Athol Cummers, much to my own satisfaction, my mother said to me, "Dear Jimmie, are there ony words to that tune?"—"No that ever I heard, mother."—"O man, it's a shame to her sic a good tune an' nae words till't. Gae away ben the house, like a good lad, and mak' me a verse till't." The request was instantly complied with.

2d, It was a great favourite with my kind friend, Mr R. P. Gillies, who sung it every night with great glee; and after he had done, and taken a laugh at it, he uniformly put his hand across his mouth, and made the following remark—"Well, I certainly do think it is a most illustrious song, Athol Cummers."

DUNCAN, lad, blaw the cummers,
Play me round the Athol cummers;
A' the din o' a' the drummers
Canna rouse like Athol cummers.
When I'm dowie, wet or weary,   5
Soon my heart grows light an' cheery,
When I hear the sprightly nummers
O' my dear, my Athol cummers!

When the fickle lasses vex me,
When the cares o' life perplex me,   10
When I'm fley'd wi' frightfu' rumours,
Then I lilt o' Athol cummers.
'Tis my cure for a' disasters,
Kebbits ewes an' crabbit masters,
Drifty nights an' dripping summers— 15
A' my joy is Athol cummers!

Ettrick banks an' braes are bonny,
Yarrow hills as green as ony;
But in my heart nae beauty nummers
Wi' my dear, my Athol cummers.   20
Lomond's beauty nought surpasses,
Save Breadalbane's bonny lasses;
But deep within my spirit slummers
Something sweet of Athol cummers.*

LOCK THE DOOR, LARISTON

This Border song was published in my own weekly paper, THE SPY,
March 30, 1811, and found its way into the London papers, and
partially through Britain, as the composition of my friend Mr Gray,
now in India. I never contradicted it, thinking that any body might
have known that no one could have written the song but myself.
However, it has appeared in every collection of songs with Mr Gray's
name. Although I look upon it as having no merit whatever, excepting
a jingle of names, which Sir Walter's good taste rendered popular,
and which in every other person's hand has been ludicrous, yet I
hereby claim the song as one of my own early productions,—mine
only, mine solely, and mine for ever.

Lock the door, Lariston, lion of Liddisdale,
Lock the door, Lariston, Lowther comes on,†
  The Armstrongs are flying,
  Their widows are crying,
The Castletown's burning, and Oliver's gone;   5
Lock the door, Lariston—high on the weather gleam
See how the Saxon plumes bob on the sky,
  Yeoman and carbineer,
  Billman and halberdier;
Fierce is the foray, and far is the cry.   10

* Maidens.
† For I defy the British nation
To match me at alliteration.
    Lit. Jour.

Bewcastle brandishes high his broad scimitar,
Ridley is riding his fleet-footed grey,
    Hedley and Howard there,
    Wandale and Windermere,—
Lock the door, Lariston, hold them at bay.   15
Why dost thou smile, noble Elliot of Lariston?
Why do the joy-candles gleam in thine eye?
    Thou bold Border ranger,
    Beware of thy danger—
Thy foes are relentless, determined, and nigh.   20

Jock Elliot raised up his steel bonnet and lookit,
His hand grasp'd the sword with a nervous embrace;
    "Ah, welcome, brave foemen,
    On earth there are no men
More gallant to meet in the foray or chase!   25
Little know you of the hearts I have hidden here,
Little know you of our moss-troopers' might,
    Lindhope and Sorby true,
    Sundhope and Milburn too,
Gentle in manner, but lions in fight!   30

I've Margerton, Gornberry, Raeburn, and Netherby,
Old Sim of Whitram, and all his array;
    Come all Northumberland,
    Teesdale and Cumberland,
Here at the Breaken Tower end shall the fray.   35
Scowl'd the broad sun o'er the links of green Liddis-
   dale,
Red as the beacon-light tipp'd he the wold;
    Many a bold martial eye
    Mirror'd that morning sky,
Never more oped on his orbit of gold!   40

Shrill was the bugle's note, dreadful the warrior
    shout,
Lances and halberds in splinters were borne;
      Halberd and hauberk then
      Braved the claymore in vain,
Buckler and armlet in shivers were shorn.   45
See how they wane, the proud files of the Winder-
    mere,
Howard—Ah! woe to thy hopes of the day!
      Hear the wide welkin rend,
      While the Scots' shouts ascend,
"Elliot of Lariston, Elliot for aye!"   50

THE LASS O' CARLISLE

I wrote this daftlike song off-hand one day to fill up a page of a
letter which was to go to Fraser by post, being averse to his paying
for any blank paper. I did not deem it worthy of publication any-
where else; but after its having appeared in print, why, let it have a
place here.

      I'll sing ye a wee bit sang,
        A sang i' the aulden style,
      It is of a bonny young lass
        Wha lived in merry Carlisle.
      An' O but this lass was bonny,   5
        An' O but this lass was braw,
      An' she had gowd in her coffers,
        An' that was best of a'.
        Sing hey, hickerty dickerty,
          Hickerty dickerty dear;   10
        The lass that has gowd an' beauty
          Has naething on earth to fear!

This lassie had plenty o' wooers,
   As beauty an' wealth should hae;
This lassie she took her a man,   15
   An' then she could get nae mae.
This lassie had plenty o' weans,
   That keepit her hands astir;
And then she dee'd and was buried,
   An' there was an end of her.   20
     Sing hey, hickerty dickerty,
       Hickerty dickerty dan,
     The best thing in life is to make
     The maist o't that we can!

MY LOVE SHE'S BUT A LASSIE YET

Was written at the request of Mr Thomson, to the old air bearing
that name. But after the verses were written, he would not have
them, because they were not good enough. "He did not like any
verses," he said, "that had the lines ending with O's, and joes, and
yets, &c. as they were very poor expedients for making up the measure
and rhyme." He was quite right; but what was a poor fellow to do,
tied to a triple rhyme like this?—The song was afterwards published
in the *Literary Journal*.

   MY love she's but a lassie yet,
   A lightsome lovely lassie yet;
     It scarce wad do
     To sit an' woo
   Down by the stream sae glassy yet.   5
   But there's a braw time coming yet,
   When we may gang a-roaming yet;
     An' hint wi' glee
     O' joys to be,
   When fa's the modest gloaming yet.   10

She's neither proud nor saucy yet,
She's neither plump nor gaucy yet;
    But just a jinking,
    Bonny blinking,
Hilty-skilty lassie yet.   15
But O her artless smile's mair sweet
Than hinny or than marmalete;
    An' right or wrang,
    Ere it be lang,
I'll bring her to a parley yet.   20

I'm jealous o' what blesses her,
The very breeze that kisses her,
    The flowery beds
    On which she treads,
Though wae for ane that misses her.   25
Then O to meet my lassie yet,
Up in yon glen sae grassy yet;
    For all I see
    Are nought to me,
Save her that's but a lassie yet!   30

THE WITCH O' FIFE

Another balloon song, notable for nothing save its utter madness.

HURRAY, hurray, the jade's away,
    Like a rocket of air with her bandalet!
I'm up in the air on my bonny grey mare,
    But I see her yet, I see her yet.
I'll ring the skirts o' the gowden wain   5
    Wi' curb an' bit, wi' curb an' bit;
An' catch the Bear by the frozen mane,—
    An' I see her yet, I see her yet.

Away, away, oe'r mountain an' main,
  To sing at the morning's rosy yett;   10
An' water my mare at its fountain clear,—
  But I see her yet, I see her yet.
Away, thou bonny witch o' Fife,
  On foam of the air to heave an' flit,
An' little reck thou of a poet's life,   15
  For he sees thee yet, he sees thee yet.

BIRNIEBOUZLE

It is said "the multitude never are wrong;" so be it. Well, then, this
has been a popular street song for nearly thirty years. How does
the instance justify the adage? Not well. However, bowing with
humility to the public voice, in preference to my own judgment, I
give it a place.

AIR—*Braes of Tullimett.*

WILL ye gang wi' me, lassie,
  To the braes o' Birniebouzle?
Baith the yird an' sea, lassie,
  Will I rob to fend ye.
I'll hunt the otter an' the brock,   5
The hart, the hare, an' heather cock,
An' pu' the limpet aff the rock,
  To batten an' to mend ye.

If ye'll gang wi' me, lassie,
  To the braes o' Birniebouzle,   10
Till the day you dee, lassie,
  Want shall ne'er come near ye.
The peats I'll carry in a skull,
The cod an' ling wi' hooks I'll pull,
An' reave the eggs o' mony a gull,   15
  To please my denty dearie.

Sae canty will we be, lassie,
    At the braes o' Birniebouzle,
Donald Gun and me, lassie,
    Ever sall attend ye.   20
Though we hae nowther milk nor meal,
Nor lamb nor mutton, beef nor veal,
We'll fank the porpy and the seal,
    And that's the way to fend ye.

An' ye sall gang sae braw, lassie,   25
    At the kirk o' Birniebouzle,
Wi' littit brogues an' a', lassie,
    Wow but ye'll be vaunty!
An' you sall wear, when you are wed,
The kirtle an' the Heeland plaid,   30
An' sleep upon a heather bed,
    Sae cozy an' sae canty.

If ye'll but marry me, lassie,
    At the kirk o' Birniebouzle,
A' my joy shall be, lassie,   35
    Ever to content ye.
I'll bait the line and bear the pail,
An' row the boat and spread the sail,
An' drag the larry at my tail,
    When mussel hives are plenty.   40

Then come awa wi' me, lassie,
    To the braes o' Birniebouzle;
Bonny lassie, dear lassie,
    You shall ne'er repent ye.
For you shall own a bught o' ewes,   45
A brace o' gaits, and byre o' cows,
An' be the lady o' my house,
    An' lads an' lasses plenty.

THE MOON WAS A-WANING

Is one of the songs of my youth, written long ere I threw aside the shepherd's plaid, and took farewell of my trusty colley, for the bard's perilous and thankless occupation. I was a poor shepherd half a century ago, and I have never got farther to this day; but my friends would be far from regretting this, if they knew the joy of spirit that has been mine. This was the first song of mine I ever heard sung at the piano, and my feelings of exultation are not to be conceived by men of sordid dispositions. I had often heard my strains chanted from the ewe-bught and the milking green, with delight; but I now found that I had got a step higher, and thenceforward resolved to cling to my harp, with a fondness which no obloquy should diminish,—and I have kept the resolution.—The song was first set to music and sung by Miss C. Forest, and has long been a favourite, and generally sung through a great portion of Scotland.

THE moon was a-waning,
   The tempest was over;
Fair was the maiden,
   And fond was the lover;
But the snow was so deep,   5
   That his heart it grew weary,
And he sunk down to sleep,
   In the moorland so dreary.

Soft was the bed
   She had made for her lover,   10
White were the sheets
   And embroider'd the cover;
But his sheets are more white,
   And his canopy grander,
And sounder he sleeps   15
   Where the hill foxes wander.

Alas, pretty maiden,
   What sorrows attend you!
I see you sit shivering,
   With lights at your window;   20

But long may you wait
   Ere your arms shall enclose him,
For still, still he lies,
   With a wreath on his bosom!

How painful the task   25
   The sad tidings to tell you!—
An orphan you were
   Ere this misery befell you;
And far in you wild,
   Where the dead-tapers hover,   30
So cold, cold and wan
   Lies the corpse of your lover!

THE ANCIENT BANNER

This song was written for, and sung at, the great football match at
Carterhaugh, on the 5th of December, 1815, when the old tattered
banner of Buccleuch was displayed at the head of the combatants.
It was the first rallying standard of the clan, and is very ancient.

AND hast thou here, like hermit grey,
   Thy mystic characters unroll'd,
O'er peaceful revellers to play,
   Thou emblem of the days of old!
Or com'st thou with the veteran's smile,   5
   Who deems his day of conquest fled,
Yet loves to view the bloodless toil
   Of sons whose sires he often led?

Not such thy peaceable intent,
   When over Border waste and wood,   10
On foray and achievement bent,
   Like eagle on his path of blood.

Symbol to ancient valour dear,
   Much has been dared and done for thee;
I almost weep to see thee here,   15
   And deem thee raised in mockery.

But no—familiar to the brave,
   'Twas thine thy gleaming moon and star
Above their manly sports to wave,
   As free as in the field of war;   20
To thee the faithful clansman's shout,
   In revel as in rage, was dear—
The more beloved in festal rout,
   The better fenced when foes were near.

I love thee for the olden day,   25
   The iron age of hardihood,
The rather that thou led'st the way
   To peace and joy through paths of blood;
For were it not the deeds of weir,
   When thou wert foremost in the fray,   30
We had not been assembled here,
   Rejoicing in a father's sway.

And even the days ourselves have known
   Alike the moral truth impress,
Valour and constancy alone   35
   Can purchase peace and happiness.
Then hail! memorial of the brave,
   The liegeman's pride, the Border's awe;
May thy grey pennon never wave
   O'er sterner field than Carterhaugh!   40

A BOY'S SONG

WHERE the pools are bright and deep,
Where the gray trout lies asleep,
Up the river and o'er the lea,
That's the way for Billy and me.

Where the blackbird sings the latest,   5
Where the hawthorn blooms the sweetest,
Where the nestlings chirp and flee,
That's the way for Billy and me.

Where the mowers mow the cleanest,
Where the hay lies thick and greenest;   10
There to trace the homeward bee,
That's the way for Billy and me.

Where the hazel bank is steepest,
Where the shadow falls the deepest,
Where the clustering nuts fall free,   15
That's the way for Billy and me.

Why the boys should drive away
Little sweet maidens from the play,
Or love to banter and fight so well,
That's the thing I never could tell.   20

But this I know, I love to play,
Through the meadow, among the hay;
Up the water and o'er the lea,
That's the way for Billy and me.

THE BITTERN'S QUAVERING
TRUMP ON HIGH

THE bittern's quavering trump on high,
   The beetle's drowsy distant hum,
Have sung the day's wild lullaby;
   And yet my Peggy is not come.

The golden primrose from the wood,   5
   The scented hawthorn's snowy flower,
Mixed with the laurel buds, I've strew'd,
   Deep in my Peggy's woodland bower.

O! come my love, the branches link,
   Above our bed of blossoms new;   10
The stars behind their curtains wink,
   To spare thine eyes so soft and blue.

No human eye, nor heavenly gem,
   With envious smile our bliss shall see,
The mountain ash his diadem   15
   Shall spread to shield the dews from thee.

O! let me hear thy fairy tread,
   Come gliding through the broomwood still;
Then on my bosom lean thy head,
   Till dawning crown the distant hill.   20

And I will watch thy witching smile,
   List what has caus'd thy long delay,
And kiss thy melting lips the while,
   Till die the sweet reproof away.

WAT O' BUCCLEUCH

SOME sing with devotion
Of feats on the ocean,
And nature's broad beauties in earth and in skies;
Some rant of their glasses,
And some of the lasses,   5
And these are twa things we maun never despise.
But down with the praises
Of lilies and daisies,
Of posies and roses the like never grew:
That flimsy inditing   10
That poets delight in,
They've coined for a havering half-witted crew.

CHORUS

But join in my chorus,
Ye blades o' the Forest,
We'll lilt of our muirs and our mountains of blue;   15
And hollow for ever,
Till a' the town shiver,
The name of our master, young Wat o' Buccleuch.

Of Douglas and Stuart,
We'd mony a true heart,   20
Wha stood for auld Scotland in dangers enew;
And Scots wha kept order
So lang on the Border,
Then wha heardnae tell o' the Wats o' Buccleuch?
Now all these old heroes,   25
Of helms and monteros,
O wha wad believe that the thing could be true;

In lineage unblighted,
And blood are united,
In our noble master, young Wat o' Buccleuch. 30
       Then join in my chorus, &c.

In old days of wassail,
Of chief and of vassal,
O these were the ages of chivalry true,
    Of reif and of rattle, 35
    Of broil and of battle,
When first our auld forefathers follow'd Buccleuch.
    They got for their merit,
    What we still inherit,
Those green tow'ring hills and low valleys of dew, 40
    Nor feared on their mailings
    For hornings or failings,
The broad sword and shield paid the rents of Buc-
    cleuch.
       Then join in my chorus, &c.

From that day to this one, 45
    We've lived but to bless them,
To love and to trust them as guardians true;
    May Heaven protect then,
    And guide and direct then,
This stem of the gen'rous old house of Buccleuch! 50
    The Wats were the callans,
    That steadied the balance,
When strife between kinsmen and Borderers grew;
    Then here's to our scion,
    The son of the lion, 55
The Lord of the Forest, the Chief of Buccleuch.

CHORUS

Then join in my chorus,
Ye lads of the Forest,
With lilt of our muirs and our mountains of blue,
And hallow for ever,   60
Till a' the tow'rs shiver,
The name of our Master, young Wat of Buccleuch.

SELECT BIBLIOGRAPHY

POEMS

The following is a chronological list of Hogg's main books of poetry:

Scottish Pastorals, poems, songs, etc. Edinburgh, 1801.
The Mountain Bard. Edinburgh and London, 1807.
The Forest Minstrel. Edinburgh and London, 1810.
The Queen's Wake. Edinburgh and London, 1813.
The Queen's Wake. 'Third' edition. Edinburgh and London, 1814.
The Pilgrims of the Sun. Edinburgh and London, 1815.
Mador of the Moor. Edinburgh and London, 1816.
The Poetic Mirror. London and Edinburgh, 1816.
The Poetic Mirror. Second edition. London and Edinburgh, 1817.
The Jacobite Relics of Scotland. Edinburgh and London, 1819.
The Queen's Wake. 'Fifth' edition. Edinburgh and London, 1819.
The Jacobite Relics of Scotland, Second Series. Edinburgh and London, 1821.
The Mountain Bard. 'Third' edition. Edinburgh, London and Glasgow, 1821.
The Poetical Works of James Hogg. 4 vols. Edinburgh and London, 1822.
Queen Hynde. A poem, in six books. London and Edinburgh, 1825.
Songs, by the Ettrick Shepherd. Edinburgh and London, 1831.
A Queer Book. Edinburgh and London, 1832.

The most important posthumous editions of Hogg's poems are:

The Poetical Works of the Ettrick Shepherd. 5 vols. Glasgow, Edinburgh, and London, 1838–40.
The Works of the Ettrick Shepherd. Edited by the Rev. Thomas Thomson. 2 vols. London, Glasgow, and Edinburgh, 1865.

Information on separate printings in periodicals, etc., is given in the bibliographical works listed below.

BIOGRAPHY AND CRITICISM

E. C. Batho, *The Ettrick Shepherd*. Cambridge, 1927.

D. Carswell, *Sir Walter: A Four-part Study in Biography*. London, 1930.

G. Douglas, *James Hogg*. Edinburgh and London, 1899.

Mrs. Garden [*née* Mary Gray Hogg], *Memorials of James Hogg*. London, 1885.

L. Simpson, *James Hogg. A Critical Study*. Edinburgh and London, 1962.

A. L. Strout, *The Life and Letters of James Hogg*, vol. i (1770–1825). Lubbock, Texas, 1946. [No more published.]

BIBLIOGRAPHICAL WORKS

E. C. Batho's *Ettrick Shepherd*—listed above—contains a detailed bibliography. The present edition owes a great deal to Miss Batho's thoroughness. Other important contributions to the subject are:

W. D. Hogg, 'The First Editions of the Writings of James Hogg', *Publications of the Edinburgh Bibliographical Society*, vol. xii (1924).

E. C. Batho, 'Notes on the Bibliography of James Hogg', *The Library*, fourth series, vol. xvi (1936).

COMMENTARY

ABBREVIATIONS

Batho   Edith C. Batho, *The Ettrick Shepherd*, Cambridge, 1927.

Domestic Manners   Hogg, *Domestic Manners of Sir Walter Scott*, Stirling, 1909.

Songs   *Songs, by the Ettrick Shepherd*, Edinburgh, London, 1831.

Works   *The Works of the Ettrick Shepherd*, edited by the Rev. T. Thomson, 2 vols., London 1865.

THE TEXT

This edition seeks to present a text which reflects Hogg's final intentions, and its text is based on a collation of the early printed editions, of the Hogg holographs in the National Library of Scotland, and of early printings in periodicals. A collation of the early texts shows that Hogg revised many of his poems extensively, in spite of the fact some passages in his *Autobiography* imply that this was not his practice. His revisions include the addition and omission of extended passages, as well as changes in wording.

Hogg's most important revisions were his alteration of the ending of 'The Witch of Fife' (see below), and his complete re-casting of the language of 'Kilmeny' and 'Ringan and May'. In these poems the change from antique to modern Scots is accomplished mainly by means of alterations in spelling, but a few Scots usages are anglicized in addition. Thus the 'leifu mayde' of Kilmeny's vision in heaven becomes a 'guardian maid'. On the other hand, Hogg's revisions of his songs for the 1831 collection show some movement from English to Scots, although a few changes in the opposite direction also occur. It should be emphasized, however, that Hogg's movement between Scots and English in his revisions was comparatively slight, and it does not appear to have been systematic.

Hogg was at various times under pressure to bowdlerize his work—for example his periodical *The Spy* lost half its subscribers because

its third number contained a story which was considered to be *risqué*.
However, the poems in the present selection contain only two revisions
which can be taken as concessions to the sensibilities of his public—
the alteration in 'O, Jeannie, there's Naething to Fear ye' of the
lovers' woodland 'bed' to a woodland 'walk', and the omission of a
stanza in 'M'Lean's Welcome' (see below).

Hogg revised *The Queen's Wake* and several of his songs with
obvious care, and in these poems he shows a concern for detail sur-
prising in a man who claimed to despise revision. His attempts at
making detailed improvements were by and large successful. One
example that might be quoted is the substitution of 'twilight sea'
for 'silver sea' in l. 289 of 'Kilmeny'.

A list of all the substantive variants in the early texts of Hogg's
poetry would be very bulky, and an edition of a selection of the
poems is not an appropriate place for the publication of such a list.
However, a selection of the more important variants is given below.
In addition the Commentary gives details of the history of the text
of each poem, and indicates the basis of the text of the present edition.

THE QUEEN'S WAKE

Text: The first three editions of this poem were published by Goldie,
the first two in 1813 and the third in 1814. The fourth edition—1814
—was published by Blackwood, who also published the fifth and
sixth editions (both 1819). The poem was reprinted in 1822 as vol. 1 of
Constable's four-volume edition of Hogg's *Poetical Works*. Goldie's
second edition is in fact a reissue of the first edition, while the fourth
edition is a reissue of the copies of the third which remained unsold
after Goldie's bankruptcy in 1814. The sixth edition is a reissue of
the fifth, and the 1822 edition is simply a page-for-page reprint of
the fifth.

The third edition contains some major revisions, the most impor-
tant being a change in the ending of 'The Witch of Fife' (see below),
and the 'translation' of 'Kilmeny' from Hogg's mock-antique Scots
into modern Scots. The fifth edition contains alterations which are
less extensive, but which obviously result from a careful authorial
revision. This text clearly represents Hogg's final intentions, and it
has been followed in the present edition. Some of Hogg's more im-
portant revisions should perhaps be described in detail. Lines 269–70
of the 'Introduction' and ll. 7–14 of the description of the Eighth
Bard appear for the first time in the fifth edition. In the first edition

'The Witch of Fife' ends at l. 272, and the words spoken by the old man in ll. 265–72 appear as part of the narrative. In 'Kilmeny' ll. 185–96 and 240–1 do not appear in the first edition. Other variants in this poem include:

ll. 199–200 The first edition has one line only—

> And mony a mortyl toyling sore,

208–9 Not in the first edition, which has instead—

> But ther cam ane leman out of the west,
> To woo the ledy that he luvit best;
> And he sent ane boy her herte to prove,
> And scho took him in, and scho callit him love;
> But quhan to her breist he gan to cling,
> Scho dreit the payne of the serpentis sting.

'Introduction'

l. 14 *lone Saint Mary's side.* St. Mary's Loch, in Ettrick Forest. See Hogg's poem 'St Mary of the Lows'.

56–7 *When Caledon, with look severe*
Saw Beauty's hand her sceptre bear.

This refers to the reign of Mary Queen of Scots, which was overshadowed by the conflicts of the Scottish Reformation.

391–402 The feelings of the rustic bards on their arrival in Edinburgh no doubt reflect Hogg's own feelings when he came to the city to attempt to win literary fame.

435–46 The 'gay and simpering man' is Rizzio, the Italian courtier who sings 'Malcom of Lorn', the first song of the Wake. Hogg contrasts his effeminate 'flowery lay' with the virile Scottish songs that follow.

The Eighth Bard

The places mentioned in the description of the eighth bard are all situated near Loch Leven, in Fife.

'The Witch of Fife'

l. 40 *the Lommond height.* The Lomond Hills overlook Loch Leven, the home of the Eighth Bard.

105 *Doffrinis.* The Dovre Fjeld mountain range in Norway.

272 In the original version the poem ends at this point, and the old man actually is 'burnit skin and bone'. (See above.) Sir Walter

Scott persuaded Hogg to change this ending, which did indeed jar with the comic tone of the poem. Hogg had this in mind when he wrote, 'I was indebted to [Scott] for the most happy and splendid piece of humorous ballad poetry which I ever wrote.' (*Domestic Manners*, p. 106.)

The Thirteenth Bard

The places named in the description of the thirteenth Bard are all in the vicinity of Loch Earn, in Perthshire.

'Kilmeny'

l. 2 *Duneira*. Dunira is situated to the east of Loch Earn. It can be approached from the loch along the glen of the River Earn.

29–32 A parallel use of the birch as an image of heavenly beauty can be found in the ballad, 'The Wife of Usher's Well'.

52–6   *In yon green-wood there is a waik,*
         And in that waik there is a wene,
         And in that wene there is a maike,
         That neither has flesh, blood, nor bane;
         And down in yon green-wood he walks his lane.

This difficult passage has been discussed convincingly by James Logie Robertson ('Hugh Haliburton') in his *Furth in Field* (London, 1894), p. 111–15. Robertson writes: 'There can be no doubt that "wene" is Hogg's form of the good old word "wane" or "wonne". "Wane" is the spelling in Henryson's fine poem, "The Borrowstoun Mous and the Landwart Mous". The field mouse's home. . . was "a simple wane" . . . Clearly, then, Hogg's "wene" stands for "dwelling".' Robertson goes on to suggest that 'maike' is a form of the Scots word 'mak' or 'make', that is, 'match' or 'mate', and that the maike in the wene is in fact the 'meek and reverend fere' who has watched over the world 'since the banquet of time' in search of a pure and sinless virgin (70 ff.). Robertson then suggests that 'waik' 'may be connected with the word "wake", signifying a "ward", or "district to watch over"'; or, again, it may be Hogg's form for "walk", with much the same meaning.'

There is no doubt that this passage in 'Kilmeny' is an echo of a passage in the old ballad 'Erlinton':

                In my bower, Willie, there is a wane,
                  An in the wane there is a wake ;
                But I will come to the green woods
                  The morn, for my ain true-love's sake.

'Wane' can mean a room or apartment in a house, as well as the house itself, and in 'Erlinton' it is used in the former sense. The 'wake' in 'Erlinton' is a watch, that is a number of people set to keep watch over the lady who is speaking. The lines quoted above are from the A-version of 'Erlinton' in F. J. Child's *English and Scottish Popular Ballads,* a version originally sent by Hogg to Scott through William Laidlaw for inclusion in *The Minstrelsy of the Scottish Border.* (See Batho, p. 19 and Child's note on his A-version.)

131 *The stream of life.* Cf. Revelation 22: 161 ff. This section of 'Kilmeny' probably owes something to Ramsay's poem 'The Vision'.

181 *A lovely land.* The land is Scotland.

202–17 The lady is Mary Queen of Scots, and this section of the poem presents a pageant of her life. The lion represents Scotland, and the bedeman represents the Reformed Church and its supporters.

220–9 This section of the poem deals with the reign of Mary's son, James VI. The early years of James's reign were marred by conflicts with the Protestant nobles, but by the time of the Union of the Crowns (when the lion was 'crowned with the rose and the clover leaf'), James had been able to establish his authority fairly firmly.

The syntax of these lines is rather involved, and perhaps it is worth mentioning that it is the carle, not the lion, who gecks at heaven in l. 228.

236–55 These lines refer to the French Revolution, and the events which followed it. The eagle represents France, the lion Britain.

295 Cf. Isaiah 11: 6, 8–9. 'The wolf also shall dwell with the lamb, and the leopard shall lie down with the kid; and the calf and the young lion and the fatling together; and a little child shall lead them . . . And the sucking child shall play on the hole of the asp, and the weaned child shall put his hand on the cockatrice' den. They shall not hurt nor destroy in all my holy mountain; for the earth shall be full of the knowledge of the Lord, as the waters cover the sea.' Compare also Isaiah 45: 17–18, 25.

'Conclusion'

The geographical references relate to the area around St. Mary's Loch.

THE POETIC MIRROR

Hogg hoped to raise money by collecting and publishing in one volume poems by each of the 'living bards of Britain'. He was disappointed by the response to his requests for poems, and in 1816 he resolved to write a number of poems 'completely in the style of each poet'. Hogg continues in his *Autobiography* (*Works*, vol. 2, p. 453):

'I set to work with great glee, as the fancy had struck me, and in a few days I finished my imitations of Wordsworth and Lord Byron.'

A number of the poems in *The Poetic Mirror*, including the 'Scott' piece 'Wat o' the Cleuch', reflect Hogg's original intention to write 'completely in the style of each poet'. In some of the poems, however—and in particular in the 'Wordsworth' ones—a strong element of parody is introduced. Indeed, Hogg remarks in the *Autobiography* that 'had the imitations of Wordsworth been less of a caricature, the work might have passed, for a season at least, as the genuine productions of the authors themselves, whose names were prefixed to the several poems' (p. 454).

Hogg's desire to parody Wordsworth can no doubt be traced back to his resentment over an incident that occurred during one of his visits to Rydal Mount. He writes in his *Autobiography* (p. 464) that in his dealings with Wordsworth he 'never met with anything but the most genuine kindness; therefore people have wondered why I should have indulged in caricaturing his style in the "Poetic Mirror". I have often regretted that myself; but it was merely a piece of ill-nature at an affront which I conceived had been put on me. It was the triumphal arch scene. . . It chanced one night, when I was there, that there was a resplendent arch across the zenith, from the one horizon to the other, of something like the aurora borealis, but much brighter. . . When word came into the room of the splendid meteor, we all went out to view it; and, on the beautiful platform at Mount Ryedale, we were all walking, in twos and threes, arm-in-arm, talking of the phenomenon, and admiring it. Now, be it remembered, that Wordsworth, Professor Wilson, Lloyd, De Quincey, and myself, were present, besides several other literary gentlemen, whose names I am not certain that I remember aright. Miss Wordsworth's arm was in mine, and she was expressing some fears that the splendid stranger might prove ominous, when I, by ill luck, blundered out the following remark, thinking that I was saying a good thing:—"Hout, me'm! it is neither mair nor less than joost a treeumphal airch, raised in honour of the meeting of the poets."

' "That's not amiss—eh? eh?—that's very good", said the Professor, laughing. But Wordsworth, who had De Quincey's arm, gave a grunt, and turned on his heel, and leading the little opium-chewer aside, he addressed him in these disdainful and venomous words:— "Poets? poets? What does the fellow mean? Where are they?"

'Who could forgive this? For my part I never can, and never will!

I admire Wordsworth; as who does not, whatever they may pretend? but for that short sentence I have a lingering ill-will at him which I cannot get rid of. It is surely presumption in any man to circumscribe all human excellence within the narrow sphere of his own capacity. The "*Where are they*?" was too bad! I have always some hopes that De Quincey was *leeing*, for I did not myself hear Wordsworth utter the words.'

The text of the first edition—1816—has been followed. Both the second edition—1817—and the version of the 1822 *Poetical Works* introduce some slight variations in the text, but these can safely be attributed to the printer. Three alterations have been made in the accidentals of the text (see below). The names of the poets parodied were listed in the table of contents of the first edition, but were not printed with the texts of the poems.

'The Flying Tailor'

l. 145 The first edition reads: bankruptcy,

181 *Author of the Isle of Palms*. That is, John Wilson ('Christopher North'). Wilson, whose reputation as a poet was based on 'The Isle of Palms', was noted for exceptional athletic prowess.

288–92 These lines refer to the unfavourable reviews which Wordsworth's poetry received in a number of periodicals, and in particular to Jeffrey's well-known criticisms of Wordsworth in *The Edinburgh Review*.

'James Rigg'

l. 89 The first edition reads: spake,

208 The first edition reads: cheviot

SUPERSTITION, VERSES TO LADY ANNE SCOTT, and THE MERMAID

Hogg writes in his *Autobiography* that in 1814 he began to prepare 'a volume of romantic poems, to be entitled "Midsummer Night Dreams" ' (*Works*, vol. 2, p. 451). 'Superstition', 'Connel of Dee', and 'The Pilgrims of the Sun' were written for this volume, but on the advice of a friend, James Park, Hogg decided to publish 'Pilgrims' as a separate work. In 1815 *Pilgrims* was published by Blackwood, with 'Superstition' included at the end of the volume.

Hogg later came to regret this decision, and in vol. 2 of his *Poetical Works* (1822) he carried out his original scheme for a volume of

Midsummer Night Dreams (see p. 334 of that volume). 'Superstition', 'The Mermaid', and 'Verses to Lady Anne Scott' are among the poems included in the 1822 volume.

'Superstition'

The 1822 text follows the text of *Pilgrims* closely, but it introduces a few variants in accidentals which can be attributed to the printer. There is also one substantive variant, which seems to reflect an authorial correction. This occurs in l. 224, where the 1822 text substitutes 'meet' for the earlier text's 'find'. In the *Pilgrims* text the compositor's eye was no doubt caught by 'find' in l. 226, and the 1822 reading has been adopted. Apart from this the text of *Pilgrims* has been followed.

ll. 115 ff. In a note on 'Old David' in *The Queen's Wake*, Hogg writes that 'never, in the most superstitious ages, was the existence of witches, or the influence of their diabolical power, more firmly believed in, than by the inhabitants of the mountains of Ettrick Forest at the present day. Many precautions and charms are used to avert this influence, and scarcely does a summer elapse in which there are not some of the most gross incantations practiced, in order to free flocks and herds from the blasting power of these old hags' (*The Queen's Wake*, 5th edition (1819), p. 356).

126 *Is cut above the breath*, This phrase was used of a cut in the shape of a cross made in a witch's forehead. Such a cut was supposed to rob the witch of her power.

'Verses to Lady Anne Scott'

This poem was first published as the dedication to *The Brownie of Bodsbeck*, a novel by Hogg which deals sympathetically with the Covenanters. The superstitions of Ettrick Forest play a large part in this novel. Lady Anne Scott was the eldest daughter of Charles, fourth Duke of Buccleuch. Hogg received generous financial help from the Buccleuch family on more than one occasion.

The *Brownie* was published in 1818, and in the same year the poem was reprinted with some slight inaccuracies in *Blackwood's* vol. 4. It was again reprinted in the 1822 *Poetical Works*, and a version with some revisions appeared in 1832 as the dedication to Hogg's *Altrive Tales*. The most significant alteration in 1832 was the insertion of ll. 171–4, but a number of more minor changes were also made. The 1832 text has therefore been followed. The title of the poem is taken from the 1822 *Poetical Works*.

ll. 77 ff. The Buccleuch family, being Episcopalians, would of course tend to sympathize with the Royalists rather than with the Covenanters. Hogg, like his parents, was a Presbyterian.

'The Mermaid'

This poem is one of Hogg's many imitations of the style of the old ballads. It was first published in 1819 in *The Edinburgh Magazine*, vol. 4, and was republished with extensive revisions in the 1822 *Poetical Works*. Hogg published ll. 65–96 as a separate song in *A Border Garland* [1819] and in the 1831 *Songs*. The 1831 text introduces some comparatively minor revisions, but Hogg would not necessarily have adopted these revisions if he had been republishing the whole ballad. The 1822 text has therefore been followed. From l. 89 to the end the text of *The Edinburgh Magazine* reads—

> No more I'll come at gloaming tide
> By this green shore to hover,
> And see the maid cling to the side
> Of her dismayed lover;
> To meet the fairy by the bower,
> The kelpy by the river,
> Or brownie by the baron's tower,
> O vanish'd all for ever!

> Still my lov'd lake from fading day
> The purple gleam shall borrow,
> And heath-fowl from his mountain grey
> Sing to the dawn good morrow!
> But on a land so dull and drear
> No joy hath my attendance;
> Fled all the scenes in Scotia dear,
> When fled her independence!

> In dome beneath the water springs
> No end hath my sojourning;
> And to this land of fading things
> Far hence be my returning.
> I leave this grave, and glassy deep,
> A long last farewell taking;
> Lie still, my love, lie still, and sleep,
> Thy day is near the breaking!

LINES TO SIR WALTER SCOTT, BART.

Scott's baronetcy was conferred in the spring of 1820, and this poem
was written to mark the occasion. Hogg refers in the poem to his
first meeting with Scott, the meeting which began their long friend-
ship. Scott visited Hogg's parents at their home, and heard Mrs.
Hogg sing 'Auld Maitland'. Hogg had sent a copy of this ballad to
Scott for inclusion in *The Minstrelsy of the Scottish Border*, but Scott
suspected that part of the poem was forged. When he heard Mrs.
Hogg sing it, however, he became convinced that the ballad was
genuine. A full account of this meeting, and of the visit of Scott and
Hogg to Rankleburn on the following day, is given in the *Domestic
Manners*, p. 1 ff. The poem is reprinted from the 1822 *Poetical Works*,
the only text to be published in Hogg's lifetime.

HYMN TO THE DEVIL

This poem has never before been published in a collection of Hogg's
poetry, although it has many of the virtues of the better-known
Village of Balmaquhapple. It was first published in 1822 as part of
Hogg's novel *The Three Perils of Man*, and was reprinted as a
separate poem in 1825 in *Blackwood's* vol. 17. The two texts are
very similar, although in l. 27 the *Blackwood's* version reads 'pleasure'
for the earlier text's 'treasure'—a variant no doubt caused by a
printer's error. The poem was not included in *The Siege of Roxburgh*,
an extensively revised version of *The Three Perils of Man* published
in the 1837 edition of Hogg's *Tales and Sketches*. The earlier text,
that of *The Three Perils of Man*, has been followed.

RINGAN AND MAY

The first version of this poem—published in 1825 in *Blackwood's* vol.
17—was written in Hogg's archaic language, but in 1832 a text
'translated' into modern Scots was published in *A Queer Book*. The
language of the original version lends some support to the suggestion
in the Introduction that *Ringan and May* shows the influence of
Henryson's *Robin and Makene*. The poem has been reprinted from
A Queer Book, as that text clearly represents Hogg's final intentions.

ST MARY OF THE LOWS

Hogg called St. Mary's Loch 'that beloved lake, which if I have not
rendered classical, has not been my blame'. (*Songs*, p. 224.) The

Yarrow flows from St. Mary's Loch, which is situated at the heart of the Border country. The poem was first published in 1829 in F. Shoberl's annual *Forget Me Not*, and was republished in 1832 in *A Queer Book* with the omission of the final stanza. Some minor authorial revisions were also made, and the text of *A Queer Book* has been followed. The final stanza of the *Forget Me Not* text reads as follows:

> Farewell, dear shade! this heart is broke
> By pang which no allayment knows;
> Uprending feelings have awoke
> Which never more can know repose.
> O, lone St. Mary of the Lows,
> Thou hold'st a treasure in thy breast,
> That, where unfading beauty glows,
> Must smile in everlasting rest.

ll. 1–2 The ruins of St. Mary's Church, anciently known as 'the kirk of St. Mary of the Lows', overlook the loch.

33 *Grieve*. The Revd. Walter Grieve, a minister of the Reformed Presbyterian Church, who lived in Ettrick after retiring from the ministry. Grieve's son John was one of Hogg's intimate friends.

THE MONITORS

Reprinted from *Blackwood's* vol. 30, 1831. The poem was not published again in Hogg's lifetime.

l. 24 *Hainault scythe*. Hainault is a region on the border of France and Belgium, situated between the Scheldt and Sambre rivers. The Hainault or Flemish scythe is an agricultural implement midway between the sickle and the scythe.

69–72 In 1815 the Duke of Buccleuch gave Hogg the farm of Altrive Lake, rent free, for life. This did much to relieve Hogg from the financial troubles which recurred throughout his life.

81–3 *The Young Shepherd. . . the young ladies o' the Lake*. That is, Hogg's son and his four daughters.

SONGS

Several of Hogg's songs were included in his early books of poetry, and many were published in periodicals and in collections of Scottish songs. Some appeared separately as 'sheets', but most of these are now lost. When he was about sixty years old Hogg collected, revised, and annotated a selection of his songs, and these were published in book form in 1831. Part of the MS. of this book survives in MS. 4805 in the National Library of Scotland. The printed text does not follow the MS. exactly; there are some substantive variants in the songs themselves, and several in Hogg's notes. It is obvious that Hogg was himself responsible for many of these revisions. The 1831 MS. is very lightly punctuated, and indeed some songs are completely without punctuation, but the punctuation of the printed text would no doubt receive Hogg's approval at the proof stage. In view of all this, songs included in the 1831 collection have been reprinted from the 1831 printed text.

The songs have been printed in the order in which they appeared in 1831, and the layout of Hogg's annotations in that edition has also been followed. Three songs not included in 1831 have been added at the end of the sequence. Most of Hogg's revisions for the 1831 collection are confined to comparatively minor matters, but in a few poems the alterations are more extensive, and indeed 'Doctor Monroe' is almost entirely rewritten. These extensive revisions are indicated in the following notes.

'Donald MacDonald'

This song was written c. 1799, when an invasion of Britain by Napoleon was widely feared. There are a number of references in the song to the political situation of that period. 'Donald MacDonald' was first published c. 1801 as a broadside, but no copies survive. It was included in the 1807 edition of *The Mountain Bard*, and also in *The Forest Minstrel*, 1810. A MS. version dated 1803 is preserved in the National Library of Scotland (MS. acc. 4213). These three early texts are generally similar in character, although some variation does occur. The main alteration in 1831 is the omission of a stanza, but a number of more minor changes are also made. The stanza omitted in 1831 reads in the 1803 MS. text:

> Last year we we [sic] were wonderfu' canty
>   Our Friends & our Country to see;
> But since the proud Consul's turn'd Vaunty
>   We'll meet him by Land and by Sea.
> Wherever a Clan is disply'd
>   Wherever Our King has a Foe;

He'll quickly see Donald M'Donald
Wi's Highland-men all in a raw
  Guns and Pistols an' a,
  Pistols and Guns an' a
We'll quickly see Donald M'Donald
  Wi' Guns and Pistols an' a.

This stanza also appears, with small variations, in *The Mountain Bard* and *The Forest Minstrel*.

ll. 13 ff. The references to Bonnie Prince Charlie and King George reflect Hogg's very frequent use of Jacobite themes in his songs.

41 The 1831 reading is 'Garny', but as this appears to be a printer's error it has been replaced with 'Gairy', the reading of the 1831 MS. and of the earlier texts.

'Bonnie Prince Charlie'

First published in *A Border Garland* [1819], an edition of nine of Hogg's songs. A later undated edition of this work—*The Border Garland*—contained twelve songs. The Edinburgh Public Library copy of this later edition has been missing for some years, and I have been unable to trace another copy.

'The Skylark'

Printed in *A Border Garland*, and again in 1828 in F. Shoberl's annual, *Forget Me Not*. Two MS. versions—one dated 1816—are preserved in the National Library of Scotland. The texts are not identical, but there are no major variants.

'The Noctes Sang'

First published in 1825 in *Blackwood's* vol. 17. Hogg was unable to include ll. 16–25 in 1831, as his note to the song makes clear. These lines have been supplied from *Blackwood's*.

l. 2 *the Blue an' the Yellow*. *The Edinburgh Review*, which had a blue and yellow cover, and which was the Whig rival of the Tory *Blackwood's Magazine*.

10 *The brand of auld Geordie Buchanan*. The cover of *Blackwood's* carried a head of George Buchanan.

'O, Jeannie, there's Naething to Fear ye!'

Included in *A Border Garland*. The most noteworthy revision in 1831 is the substitution of 'walk' for 'bed' in l. 17.

'The Village of Balmaquhapple'

Published in 1826 in *Blackwood's* vol. 19, as part of the 'Noctes Ambrosianae'. Hogg reprinted some dialogue from the 'Noctes' in 1831. The 1831 text has no punctuation after 'it' in l. 22, and this is clearly an error. *Blackwood's* has a semi-colon, and this punctuation has been adopted.

'When the Kye Comes Hame'

First published in 1822 in Hogg's novel *The Three Perils of Man*. A revised version appeared in 1823 in *Blackwood's* vol. 13, and further revisions were made in 1831. The order of the stanzas varies considerably in the three texts. In *The Three Perils* the fourth stanza of 1831 is omitted, while 1831's fifth stanza appears after 1831's sixth and seventh stanzas. *The Three Perils* has a final stanza not included in 1831:

> Away wi' fame and fortune,
>   What comfort can they gie?
> And a' the arts that prey
>   On man's life and libertye;
> Gie me the highest joy
>   That the heart of man can frame,
> My bonny, bonny lassie,
>   When the kye come hame.

Blackwood's has the same final stanza as *The Three Perils*, and omits the last two stanzas of 1831. It inserts the following lines between 1831's fourth and fifth stanzas:

> Then the eye shines sae bright, the hale soul to beguile,
>   There's love in every whisper, and joy in every smile:
> O wha wad choose a crown, wi' its perils and its fame,
>   And miss a bonny lassie when the kye come hame?

Blackwood's is printed throughout in four-line stanzas, each line comprising two lines from the other texts.

In addition, the text of *The Three Perils* varies from 1831 as follows:

ll. 1–4

> Come tell me a' you shepherds
>   That love the tarry woo',
> And tell me a' you jolly boys
>   That whistle at the plow,

58–62   Then the eye shines sae bright,
    The hale soul to beguile,
    There's love in every whisper,
    And joy in every smile.

'M'Lean's Welcome'

Published in 1821 in *The Jacobite Relics* Second Series, and republished *c.* 1824 in vol. 5 of R. A. Smith's *Scottish Minstrel* with the omission of the third stanza. This stanza, which was also omitted in 1831, reads—

Come o'er the stream, Charlie, &c.
O'er heath-bells shall trace you the maids to embrace you,
And deck your blue bonnet with flowers of the brae;
And the loveliest Mari in all Glen-M'Quarry
Shall lie in your bosom till break of the day.

The 1831 *Songs* prints each line of *The Jacobite Relics* as two lines, except that l. 35 is not broken up in this way.

'When Maggy Gangs Away'

I have been unable to trace any printing earlier than 1831.

'Donald M'Gillavry'

An original song by Hogg first published in 1819 in *The Jacobite Relics* as a traditional song. In a note in that volume Hogg calls it 'one of the best songs that ever was made' and 'a capital old song, and very popular'. He solemnly gives some information about the clan M'Gillavry, and about some notable members of the clan. He suggests, however, that 'the name seems taken to represent the whole of the Scottish clans by a comical patronymic'.

l. 3 The gouk's, or cuckoo's, nest is the throne, and the cuckoo-intruder is King George. 'Gouk' can also mean 'fool', and here both senses are intended.

5–8 A 'weigh-bauk' or balance can be used to distinguish between a genuine and a counterfeit coin. It is suggested that Donald should test the claims of King James and King George in a similar way.

32–6 Many Highlanders were in a position to betray Bonnie Prince Charlie, and thus earn a large reward. None of them chose to do so.

'Charlie is my Darling'

Published in 1821 in *The Jacobite Relics*, Second Series, together with a text of the traditional version.

'Meg o' Marley'

Sung by the Shepherd in a number of the 'Noctes Ambrosianae' in *Blackwood's* vol. 19, 1826. Hogg reprinted some of the 'Noctes' dialogue in 1831.

l. 4 The 1831 text has no punctuation after 'eery'. As this is clearly an error the *Blackwood's* punctuation—a semi-colon—has been inserted.

4–8 The 'Bangor' is one of the tunes to which the Scottish Metrical Psalms are sung. The 'clerk' is the Session Clerk, who normally acted as precentor. Thus, Meg's beauty disrupts a church service at two important points—the singing of a Psalm, and the announcement of the text of the minister's sermon.

'Black Mary'

Published in 1816 in *Albyn's Anthology*, vol. 2, and again in 1828 in *The Edinburgh Literary Journal*, vol. 1.

'Love is Like a Dizziness'

An early song, published in 1810 in *The Forest Minstrel* and again in the 1822 *Poetical Works*. The most important change in 1831 is the omission of the following penultimate stanza, which is quoted from *The Forest Minstrel*—

> Were Peggy's love to hire the job,
>   An' save my heart frae breakin', O,
> I'd put a girdle round the globe,
>   Or dive in Corryvrekin, O;
> Or howk a grave at midnight dark
>   In yonder vault sae eerie, O;
> Or gang an' spier for Mungo Park
>   Through Africa sae dreary, O.

'A Witch's Chant'

This song is a revised version of dialogue spoken by witches in Hogg's play *All-Hallow-Eve*, published in vol. 1 of his *Dramatic Tales*, 1817. The revisions are not extensive.

'Auld Ettrick John'

An early song, published in 1804 in *The Scots Magazine*, vol. 66; in *The Mountain Bard*, 1807; in *The Forest Minstrel*, 1810; and in the 1822 *Poetical Works*. These texts are generally similar in character, although there is some variation. The 1831 text contains a number of more important changes. The text of *The Scots Magazine* does not contain ll. 49–56 of the 1831 version, and has instead:

> "Gude-wife', quo" John, as he sat down,
>   "I'm come to court your doughter Nell;
> An' if I die immediately,
>   She sall hae a' the gear hersel.
> An' if she chance to hae a son,
>   I'll breed him up a braw divine;
> But if ilk wiss turn out a we'an
>   There's little fear but she hae nine."
>
> Now Nelly thought, an' ay she leugh,
>   Our lads are a' for sodgers gane,
> Young Tam will kiss an' toy enough,
>   But he o' marriage tauketh nane.
> When I am laid in Johnie's bed,
>   Like hares or lav'rocks, I'll be free;
> I'll busk me braw, an' conquer a',
>   Auld Johnie's just the man for me.

The lines omitted in *The Scots Magazine* are also omitted in *The Mountain Bard* and the 1822 *Poetical Works*. *The Mountain Bard* has both the above stanzas, but the 1822 version has the first only.

'Doctor Monroe'

First published in 1810 in *The Forest Minstrel*. Apart from the first twelve lines the song was entirely rewritten in 1831, and in *The Forest Minstrel* it reads as follows from l. 13 to the end:

> "I'll bleed and I'll blister you, over and over;
>   I'll master your malady ere that I go:
> But raise up your head from below the bed cover,
>   And give some attention to Doctor Monro.
>
> If Christy had wed you, she would have misled you,
>   And laugh'd at your love with some handsome young beau.
> Her conduct will prove it; but how would you love it?"
>   "I soon would have lam'd her, dear Doctor Monro."

"Each year brings a pretty young son, or a daughter;
  Perhaps you're the father; but how shall you know?
You hugg them—her gallant is bursting with laughter"—
  "That thought's like to murder me, Doctor Monro."

"The boys cost you many a penny and shilling;
  You breed them with pleasure, with trouble, and woe:
But one turns a rake, and another a villain."—
  "My heart could not bear it, dear Doctor Monro."
"The lasses are comely, and dear to your bosom;
  But virtue and beauty has many a foe!
O think whay may happen; just nipt in their blossom!"—
  "Ah! merciful Heaven! cease, Doctor Monro.

Dear Doctor, I'll thank you to hand me my breeches;
  I'm better; I'll drink with you ere that you go;
I'll never more sicken for women or riches,
  But love my relations and Doctor Monro.
I plainly perceive, were I wedded to Christy,
  My peace and my pleasures I needs must forego."
He still lives a bachelor; drinks when he's thirsty;
  And sings like a lark, and loves Doctor Monro.

'Athol Cummers'

First published in *The Forest Minstrel*. The 1831 text contains some revisions.

'Lock the Door, Lariston'

Published in 1811 in *The Spy* no. 31, and in the 1822 *Poetical Works*. Lines 21–5 are not included in these texts, but are added in 1831. In l. 47 the 1831 MS. has 'deeds' where all the other texts have 'hopes'.

'The Lass o' Carlisle'

First published in 1830 in *Fraser's Magazine*, vol. 1.

'My Love She's But a Lassie Yet'

First published in 1830 in *The Edinburgh Literary Journal*, vol. 3.

'The Witch o' Fife'

This is a revised version of a song which appeared in Hogg's 'Dr David Dale's Account of a Grand Aerial Voyage', which was published in 1830 in *The Edinburgh Literary Journal*, vol. 3. Dr. Dale is accompanied by the Ettrick Shepherd on an outrageously improbable balloon journey, and the Shepherd sings this song as the balloon rushes upwards from the earth. The shepherd also sings a song to 'The Moon', and this poem precedes 'The Witch o' Fife' in the 1831 *Songs*. Early drafts of both songs appear in National Library of Scotland MS. 4805.

'Birniebouzle'

First published in *The Forest Minstrel*, 1810. In this version it is the lassie who speaks in the fifth stanza.

'The Moon was a-waning'

Included in the 1822 *Poetical Works*.

'The Ancient Banner'

The football match which was the occasion of this song was also the occasion of Scott's 'Lines on the Lifting of the Banner of Buccleuch'. The two poems were published together as *The Ettrick Garland*, 1815. Hogg's song was reprinted in 1815 in the *Scots Magazine*, vol. 77, and in the 1822 *Poetical Works*.

'A Boy's Song'

This song, which was not included in the 1831 collection, is reprinted from the posthumous 5-vol. edition of Hogg's *Poetical Works*, 1838–40. This is the first printed text.

'The Bittern's Quavering Trump on High'

Not included in the 1831 *Songs*. Published in *The Spy* no. 36, 1811, and in the 1822 *Poetical Works*. The song is reprinted from the earlier text, but *The Spy's* punctuation has been altered in ll. 7 and 15. The original punctuation was as follows:

l. 7 buds;
   15 ash, his diadem,

'Wat o' Buccleuch'

Not included in 1831. This song, which has been reprinted from a number of the 'Noctes Ambrosianae' in *Blackwood's* vol. 19, 1826, has never before been published in a collection of Hogg's poems. The

Shepherd says in the 'Noctes' that it was written 'for the young
Duke of Buccleuch's birthday, held at Selkirk the 25th of November
1825'. 'The young Duke' was Walter, 5th Duke of Buccleuch, son of
Duke Charles, who had given Hogg the farm of Altrive Lake in 1815.
The air of the song is given as 'Thurot's Defeat'.

GLOSSARY

aboun, above
ae, one
aft, often
aince, once
ane, one
aneath, beneath
arles, *arle*, a payment; one's deserts, a thrashing. (The singular form is unusual, but is used in *Hymn to the Devil*)
attour, over
auld, old
ava, at all

ban, to curse, swear
bannock, a thick, round, flat cake, generally of oatmeal.
bauk, balk
beal, beacon-fire kindled on a height
beetle-bee, a humming beetle
bele-fire, a large fire, or funeral pyre
ben, *n.* the best room or parlour of a house. *adv.* into the parlour, in the direction of the speaker
bide, to stay, remain
big, to build
birk, birch
bladd, a large portion of anything
blewart, the blue corn-flower
blink, to twinkle
bogle, ghost, spectre
boordly, sturdy
bothy, a primitive dwelling; a dairy-house used in summer by Highland shepherds (see *The Scottish National Dictionary*)
brainzel, to act in a violent, headlong manner
braw, worthy, excellent
breek-knee, breeches-knee
breeks, trousers

brochin, *brochan*, the plaid worn by Highlanders. (Used as a collective noun)
brock, badger
brose, porridge
brownie, a household spirit; a goblin
brume-cow, a besom of broom
bught, a sheep- or cattle-fold
burd, offspring, in a bad sense
busk, to dress; a dress
butt, verily, certainly. (Used redundantly for emphasis)

cairny, a cairn, a conical pile of stones
callan, *callant*, a stripling, a lad
cantrip, a spell, a witch's trick
canty, lively, cheerful
carena by, to be indifferent
carle, person, fellow
cauldrife, cold, chilly
cheip, to chirp
chiel, fellow
chirl, a low, melancholy sound
claught, caught
clotters, clods
cludis, clouds
cog, a wooden vessel for holding milk, etc.
corby, crow, raven, rook
cour, to cower, crouch
crack, to gossip
craigy, rocky
crouse, lively, elated
cruik-shell, a hook for suspending a pot over a fire
cummer, maiden

dadd, to strike, to career headlong
darn, to zigzag through; to hide
dawtied, treasured

dead-light, phosphorescence, supposed to appear in graveyards; a 'corpse-candle'

dee, to die

deide, death

den, glen, ravine

denty, comely

deray, disorder

dern, wild

dirl, to resound noisily

docht, could

docken, the dock

doddit, hornless

doited, foolish, in dotage

doop, to descend, droop

douffe, gloomy

douk, to plunge

doup, buttocks

dour, stern, unyielding

dover, to stun

dow, dove; a term of endearment

dowie, sad

downa, to be reluctant to

dree, to endure, undergo

dreep, to drop slowly

driche, slow, dreary

droul, in phrase 'dust and droul', dust and ashes.

Dunedin, Edinburgh

dunt, to strike bodily; to career headlong

ee, eye

ee-bree, eye-brow

een, eyes

eident, diligent, steady

eithly, easily

eldron, old

elwand, a measuring-rod

ely, to vanish gradually

ern, eagle

ether, adder

eyne, eyes

fank, to entangle, trap

fash, to trouble, vex

faurd, *p.p. adj.*, featured

fend, to provide for

fere, comrade; spouse, match, equal

ferit, afraid

ferly, to wonder

fire-flaucht, a flash of lightning

fit, foot

flee, to fly

flichter, to move quiveringly in the air

flisky, skittish

fluff, to flap

flyting, a scolding-match, a noisy and abusive quarrel; ranting abusively

forhoo, to forsake, abandon—especially of a bird deserting its nest

foughten, fought

froward, perverse

gadman, the man in charge of a plough-team

gainder, a gander

gaishen, a skeleton, an emaciated person

gait, goat

gar, to cause to

gate, street; way. In phrase 'gie him his gate'—give him his way, give him his head

gaucy, plump, large

gavelock, an iron crowbar

gear, property

geck, gaze

gettling, a little child

gin, if

girn, to complain bitterly; a snarl; a grin, a smile

glair, to glare

gledge, to glance at, look slyly at

gloaming, twilight

gloff, fear, a sudden fright; a sudden variation in the density of darkness

gor-cock, the moor-cock

gouk, a cuckoo; a fool

gove, to gaze

gowd, gold

gowl, a wide opening; to yell, howl

grat, wept

greet, to weep

grew, a greyhound

gudebrither, brother-in-law

gudeman, the master of a house

gurly, surly, rough

gysart, a mummer

halesome, wholesome
hap, to cover
haun', hand
haver, to speak nonsensically
heather-cock, the ring-ousel
hern, heron
hilty-skilty, helter-skelter
hindberry, the wild raspberry
hinny, honey
ho, stocking
holt, a wooded hill
hoody craw, the carrion crow
hoolet, owl
houf, a favourite haunt
howk, to dig
humloke, hemlock; any hollow-stemmed umbelliferous plant
hurkle, to submit

ilk, *ilka*, each, every
ingle, hearth, fireplace

javel, rascal
jink, to frolic, move nimbly
joup, a woman's skirt

keb, *used of ewes*: to bring forth a stillborn lamb
kebbuck, a whole cheese
keek, to look, peep
kelpy, water sprite
kemed, combed
ken, to know
kerlying, old woman
keust, to cast off
kirk, church
kirtle, a gown
knowes, hillocks, mounds
kye, cattle
kyth, to show, appear

laibies, flap or skirt of a coat
laird, landed proprietor
laith, loath
land, a house of different stories, let out in tenements
lane, *in phrases* its lane, his lane, etc.—alone, by itself, by himself
larry, something pulled behind (from 'lurry', to lug or pull) [?]
laup, leaped
laverock, lark

law, a hill, usually conical in shape
leal, loyal, sincere
lear, liar
leet, chosen, appointed
leifu', full of love, lovely: or perhaps a variant of *leal*, chaste (see *The Scottish National Dictionary*)
leil, loyal, sincere
leman, lover
leme, gleam; to gleam
len, to rest, recline
leugh, laughed
lick, to strike, beat
lift, the sky
lingel, to bind with shoemaker's thread
linn, the pool at the base of a waterfall; the waterfall itself
linty, the linnet
litt, to dye, blush
littand, causing to blush
lone, pasture
lowe, a blaze, flame, glow; to blaze, flame
lown, serene, gentle
lucken gowan, the globe-flower
lug, ear
lum, chimney
lythlye, with agility

mae, more
maike, mate, match, equal
mailing, the rent of a farm
marled, variegated, parti-coloured
marmalete, marmalade
maun, must
mavis, song-thrush
merk, dark
merl, blackbird
mind, to remember
minny, mother
mird, flattery
mirk, dark
moon-fern, moonwort
moot, to moult
moud, moth
mouldy, earthy
muckil, *muckle*, greatly; large, big
mump, to speak affectedly
mussel hives, mussel beds
mynde, mind; to remember

naigis, nags
neb, nose, the point of anything
needle, to move like a needle, to penetrate
neicher, *nicher*, to make a sound like a horse's whinny: to whinny
nor, than
norlan, northern
nurice, to nurse

or, before
outower, over, beyond
ower, *our*, over; too

pang, strong
pawky, shrewd, kindly, homely
pearily, *pirlie*, very small
philabeg, the leather pouch worn in front of a kilt; a kilt
pingle, a struggle for a livelihood; a turmoil
pliskie, plight
ploy, escapade
poortith, poverty
porpy, porpoise
prigg, to haggle
prinkle, to tingle
propine, a gift in recognition of services

qu-, used for 'wh-' in *The Witch of Fife* and other poems. See Commentary
quhill, till

raike, to roam, wander: a journey
reave, to steal, plunder
redd, to put out (a fire)
reek, *reike*, smoke
reif, robbery, plunder
rhame, a monotonous repetition
routh, abundance
row, to flow

scadd, to scald
schaw, *shaw*, a stalk
scour, to move quickly
sey, to try, essay
seymar, a loose upper garment
shaw, a flat piece of ground at the foot of a hill or steep bank
sheil, cottage

shill, shrill
shillfa, chaffinch
shoon, shoes
shouir, *showre*, a paroxysm; a sudden storm
sic, such
siller, silver; money
skelp, to strike
skull, a wicker basket
slee, sly
snell, keen, fierce
snool, to make abject
sock, a ploughshare
sonsy, buxom
sough, the moaning of the wind
soup, to sweep
souse, to fall suddenly, with a bump
speer, to ask
speil, to climb
stang'd, stung
starn, star
stave, a short song
stern-shot, lit. star-shot; a meteor
storm-cock, field-fare
stown, stolen
sturt, trouble, wrath
swa'd, *swawed*, rolled along
swaip, to sweep
swale, swelling wave
syde, wide, long; trailing

tangleness, indecision, fluctuation
tent, to attend to
theek, to cover with straw
thrapple, the throat
thrawn, thrown
til, *till*, to; that
tinchel, a group of men who surround a herd of deer
tine, lose
tither, the other
tod, fox
tout, to toot; to sound like a horn; to toss about
tove, to fly back
towe, string, thread
trepan, to seduce, infatuate
tuzzle, to embrace roughly

unco, exceedingly
unmeled, not meddled with, innocent

vaunty, exultant

waesome, sad
waik, ward, district to watch over; or *perhaps* walk
wain, to convey
wale, veil
warlock, wizard
warly, worldly
warst-faurd, worst-featured
wauf, to wave, flap
waul, *wawlyng*, to gaze wildly, gazing wildly
wean, child
wee, little, small
weigh-bauk, a balance

weir, war
weird, fate, significance
wene, dwelling, habitation
werde, fate
westlin, western
whilly-whaup, curlew
won, to dwell, live
woo, wool
wud, mad
wycht, wight, creature, person

yerk, to bind tightly
yett, gate
yird, earth
yorlin, yellow-hammer
yout, to roar, bellow

PRINTED IN GREAT BRITAIN
AT THE UNIVERSITY PRESS, OXFORD
BY VIVIAN RIDLER
PRINTER TO THE UNIVERSITY